THE HILL WHERE EXCELLENCE DWELLS

BE | DO | HAVE

F. SANFORD MAHR

First Edition

First Published by Production Concepts XXXVI

Copyright © by F. Sanford Mahr 2021

www.HillWhereExcellenceDwells.com
ExcellenceDwells.com

ISBN: 978-1-7368157-0-0

Also Available as an eBook:

ISBN: 978-1-7368157-1-7

DEDICATION

For my lady | my children, and their children | For my family and friends | For my fellow *"Comrade in Arms"* | For my colleagues | and for any that may be interested in these musings.

These words and whatever "sparks" or catalysts they may bring are yours to use or discard as you choose.

They are given for your nows, for those sparks that ignite your lights, to possibly illuminate your journeys.

CREDITS AND THANKS

Thanks to Dr. James DeMesa and Neil J. Cantor, 1 for
our Mastermind Alliance, (Tres Amigos) which gave birth to
the initial concept of a book project in the early 1990s

Thanks to *all* for the trails, the trials, the highs and lows,
and the sharing in exploring the wonderment of the
amazing experience called life.

November, 1995 Key West Grill
"The Mastermind Group"
Tres Amigos

Book cover photography copyright © Bruce W. Heinemann
(thefineartofliving.art)
Edited by Paul Weisser, Ph.D. (editor-writer.net)
C2 Design Group–Cover design (c2dg.com)
Michael Kwitko, initial proofreading
References and acknowledgments are made to sources
as footnoted throughout this book
www.HillWhereExcellenceDwells.com

To Life | L'Chaim | A Salut | Alla Vita
Viva la Vida

2006

THE HILL WHERE EXCELLENCE DWELLS

BE | DO | HAVE

"Excellence dwells on the hill, where negativity, worry, fear, and doubt are barred from visitation or occupancy." —*fsm*

CONTENTS

"Worse than being a conformist is being a nonconformist and conforming with nonconformity." —Solomon "Sol" Mahr

CONTENTS/APPENDIX

Appendix:

- **A Gentleman's Creed**
- **Notes to My Daughter**
- **A Medical Odyssey—Survival and Recovery**
- **Back in the Day—Interview with Rachael Mahr 2001**
- **FSM Birthday Letter—My Mother's Tree**
- **Brushstrokes on the Landscape of Life**
- **FSM Be Grateful and Proactive**
- **Eulogy for My Brother**
- **Birthday Message to My Brother**
- **Thanksgiving Is Not a Day, It Is a Way**
- **To Be a Warrior**
- **One Warrior's Recollections**
- **This Too Shall Pass: FSM Letter to RHG with Poem Following**
- **Eagles and Ducks**
- **The Good Morning Sun**

Bibliography:

Let's

let's go up high on
a hill...
stand perfectly still
touch the sky
kiss....
say hi....
and meet each other
again,
for the first time.
will you give me your word
you'll laugh with me....
we can linger for days
a night or two...
too
the way back is long
though...
surely
you must know...
surely
you must see...
there's the fog to traverse
waves of mist
invading the path....
leaving the moonlight
(sigh), behind,
until
just then....
when
the sunlight
danced in the air.
it wasn't so bad coming back,
we can go again.
no....
let's not.
let's gaze at the sky,
kiss,
say hi,
again,
for the first time

1

INTRODUCTION

When the impossible has been eliminated, all that remains, no matter how improbable, is possible.

—Sir Arthur Conan Doyle

You can see the future by standing on the shoulders of giants.

—Sir Isaac Newton

his book is a collection, if you will, of one man's journey, life lessons, thoughts, inspirations, and inquiries. It was written so that these may be shared with those select few who may desire to (a) read it, (b) consider it, (c) or pay it forward and pass it on. It is not intended to be authoritative or presented as static fact. Rather, it is dynamic, and the concepts are "sparks"[1] to hopefully empower readers to build on and ignite more "sparks" that will further illuminate their journeys.

I hope, as these pages unfold, that some of the experiences, observations, and lessons from the life of this one man, committed to the pursuit of excellence, learning, and *constant-and never-ending improvement* [C.A.N.I.],[2] resonate for the reader.

These writings are a result or byproduct of a commitment to excellence that has been derived from many experiences, external sources, alliances, and independent thought processes, some of which were garnered through Mastermind Alliances.[3] Note that a mastermind creates a whole that is much

---

[1]A concept in some Kabbalah writings.

[2]In his writings and lectures, Anthony Robbins uses *C.A.N.I.*, which is from *Kaizen*, a Japanese term that is used to describe the philosophy and science of constant and never-ending improvement or betterment or refinement. It is the idea that nothing is ever finished or declared perfect; there is always room for improvement.

[3]Mastermind Alliances are taught by Napoleon Hill in *Think and Grow Rich* (Meridian, CT: The Ralston Society, 1937).

greater than the sum of its parts. The creation of this book hopefully will benefit people who have an interest in, need for, or desire for learning and growing.

Almost all individuals who have been successful feel that they could have been even more so if they had had the benefit of a mentor—a guide to assist them and direct the courses they might have taken and the options they might have selected as they pursued their destinies. Enjoy your journey. Enjoy the process. Make today and every day thereafter special.

I believe that there is an infinitesimal amount of difference between success and failure, which is sometimes not even easily quantifiable. Furthermore, to increase your odds at achieving success, you should be committed to the metaphoric concept of "1% over 100%"[4] in everything you do. The concepts, experiences, and observations presented in this book will hopefully be contemplative, informational, and provocative of further thought and action.

BE | DO | HAVE[5]
Be — We Are
Do — We Create
Have — We Produce

---

[4]This should serve as a "spark" to readers, questioning not only what this means, but also how they can apply it to their own goals and endeavors—to not be static beings, but rather dynamic becomings.

[5]The concept of Be | Do | Have is repeated throughout this book, and explained in Chapter 4, "Success."

CHAPTER 1

THE QUESTIONS

Each now is but a moment on the trail of all nows.

—Nicholas Evans, *The Horse Whisperer*[6]

The first *few* of the following questions were presented to me many years ago by a close friend of mine, Norman Linton. I added the other two questions and thought to present them as a starting point to help frame issues of relevance and importance to any individuals who desire clarity and direction in their lives.

Going through this exercise was very enlightening and significant for me, since it helped me to better understand some of the issues and areas that required change in my own life.

The questions are as follows:

1. If you could be any age at all, what age would you choose to be?
2. What age would you be if you did not know how old you are now?
3. If you could live anywhere at all, where would you choose to live?
4. If you could have anyone at all as your mate, who would it be, or what would he or she be like?

---

[6]Nicholas Evans, *The Horse Whisperer* (New York : Delacorte Press, 1995).

5. If you could choose to be doing anything now in your life or for your life's work, what would it be?
6. If you could change any aspects of your life, what would they be?

When asking these questions of yourself and answering them honestly, keep in mind the "Serenity Prayer" as follows:

Grant me the serenity to accept the things I cannot change, the courage to change the things I can, and the wisdom to know the difference.[7]

After these questions have been answered, keeping full cognizance of what can be changed and what cannot, you need to move on to the next step, which is *to make them happen*. Begin immediately by implementing the necessary changes indicated as a part of your life. Don't try to do them all at once. Plan and stage them into your daily routine. Use the "Eating the Elephant" technique, which asks a simple question: How do you eat an elephant? The answer is, "one bite at a time."[8]

On the night before I was leaving home to become a musician at the age of 22, my father taped to my bedroom door a note that said: "Today is a new day. What will you have, success or failure? The choice is yours and only yours. It is up to you. What you are and what you become will be determined by what you do today. Once today is lost, it is lost forever, never to return. Choose success, you will be happier. Do the right thing. You know what it is."

My friend since early boyhood, Ken Kaufman, and I once paraphrased a famous quote as follows: "Average minds discuss people. Above-average minds discuss people sometimes, but more often discuss events. Superior minds discuss people sometimes, events sometimes; however, they primarily discuss ideas."

---

[7]Wikipedia, en.wikipedia.org/wiki/Serenity_Prayer/.
[8]Bill Hogan, *How Do You Eat an Elephant?: One Bite at a Time* (Plantation, FL: Llumina Press, 2011).

5

CHAPTER 2

WHY

(A work in progress started in March 1999)

He who has a why to live for can bear almost any how.

—German philosopher Friedrich Nietzsche[9]

Drink to Me.

—Pablo Picasso (1881–1973)[10]

W hy do so many things in life happen as they do? Why do some people seem to lead self-directed lives illustrated with color and vibrancy? Their palates are a vast array of color, which is applied by each of their interpretations of the life they are experiencing. Each

---

[9]En.wikipedia.org/friedrich_nietzsche/.

[10]My daughter, Rachael Sarah Mahr Pollack, introduced this saying to me. These are purported to be Pablo Picasso's last words. Perhaps they aptly address some of the answers to the questions this book poses. Life is all about living one's life as a celebration to the fullest and with *joie de vivre*, as the French say. One should always toast the way one has lived.

choice of color or color combinations then leads to a myriad of possibilities of what can be realized and created. Yet, there are other people, unfortunately in far greater numbers, who live their lives in black-and-white—perhaps with the occasional exception of a hue of gray showing up here or there. Why is it that, throughout their lives, those very same people experience others and events that seem to show up or occur at precisely the right moment when they are supposed to, or perhaps required to? If that is not recognized at the time, perhaps their paradigms are such that they are not ready to recognize, appreciate, or understand how the experience fits.[11] Are we living our lives every day as a celebration, and as such in "living color," or are we more complacent, accepting of the unchallenged ways of the masses, afraid to step outside self-defining comfort zones, and therefore relegated to live in black-and-white? It is conceivable that only those who choose to live their lives with passion and possibility, only those who embrace living in color, are able to realize when others offer new perspectives, new challenges, and new learning, even if those are offered in the form of sadness or disappointment. When those people or opportunities manifest themselves in our lives, the universe may be inviting each of us to participate in a drama, to grow as much as possible, coloring our own world with the interaction that is about to unfold.

It seems to me that the essence of our physical life is interpersonal relationships between people. This holds true whether or not we perceive the interactions with others as good, bad, or indifferent. All social interactions can be a blessing. They can be a contributory factor to making each of us the best we can be. The key is to be open and receptive. Only then can an unfolding life become an exciting process.

There are times when we make an instant connection with new people. We immediately have a pervasive sense of knowing that they are here because they are meant to be. Yet, there are other times when encountering people does not seem right at all, or perhaps the timing is just a bit off. Sometimes our interactions with them may even be confrontational, strained, adversarial, or hurtful. At other times, those interactions can be confusing, based on where we are in our lives and what else we might be feeling or experiencing. Nevertheless, in any scenario, we eventually come to realize that as people ebb and flow in our life journeys, they each bring a lesson or experience that ultimately serves our growth and development.

People who show up in our lives may come from virtually any walk of life

---

[11]There is an ancient teaching, "When the student is ready, the teacher will appear."

or circumstance. They may be our associates or colleagues, adversaries or opponents, teammates or co-workers, service providers, friends, mates, lovers, prospective mates or lovers, teachers, family members, daughters, sons, fathers, mothers, grandchildren, or even complete strangers. Regardless-of where they come from or how we encounter them, our interactions with them will affect our lives in some profound way.

Sometimes the initial result of meeting those people seems to be negative, creating hurtful, painful, or unfair experiences. At other times, our interactions with others can be challenging and confusing, forcing us to step outside our comfort zones by putting aside the paradigms that we have operated by until that point. Over time, we come to realize that without overcoming the challenges, obstacles, or hurdles that these encounters presented, we have not realized our full potential or gained the strength, wisdom, and willpower that serve us later in our lives as we transcend our baselines to higher personal levels. In essence, we become better and grow stronger by each interaction.[12] As Neale Donald Walsch said in *Conversations with God*, "It is within the seeds of adversity that self-experiences grow. It is only through relationships with other people, places, and events that one can exist as a knowable quantity, as an identifiable something in the universe. Remember, absent everything else, you are not."[13]

To loosely paraphrase the title of the movie *Close Encounters of the Third Kind*,[14] our encounters and interactions with others constitute "close encounters with the human kind." What may appear to be random chaos is actually an orderly unfolding of choice, cause, and effect. The entire universe is an ordered infrastructure in a delicate balance. It is said that when a butterfly flaps its wings in one part of the world, a rippling effect can occur in another. The book *Entanglement*, by Amir D. Aczel, addresses the field-of quantum mechanics as postulated by Einstein and his colleagues.[15] The idea they addressed is that subatomic particles are inextricably linked, and that a change in one will instantly be reflected in its counterpart, even if they are

---

[12]In *Twilight of the Idols* (1888), Friedrich Nietzsche said, "That which does not kill us makes us stronger."

[13]Neale Donald Walsch, *Conversations with God* (New York: Penguin Putnam, 1996).

[14]A Steven Spielberg movie in which aliens make contact with civilized Earth and communicate through musical tones. Close encounters of the third kind occur when there is communication between Earth and UFOs, as distinct from close encounters of the first or second kind, in which there are only UFO sightings or evidence of extraterrestrial matter.

[15]Amir D. Aczel, *Entanglement* (New York: Four Walls Eight Windows, 2001).

separated by a universe.

It is my viewpoint and the opinion of many others that nothing happens by chance or by luck. However, as will be further explained in Chapter 5, below, living one's life under the assumption that everything happens for a reason is flawed. Illness, injury, love, loss of love, lost moments of true greatness, death of a loved one, and mistakes caused by whatever reason all test the limits of our souls. Through our interactions with others and the circumstances we encounter, we are continually forging our souls. This is not unlike the way steel is forged when the intense heat of a blast furnace is applied to iron ore. Without these tests, our lives would be like a smoothly paved, straight, flat road to nowhere. The ride would be safe and comfortable, but dull and pointless. Helen Keller said, "Character cannot be developed in ease and quiet. Only through experience of trial and suffering can the soul be strengthened, ambition inspired, and success achieved."[16]

The people we meet who affect our lives help us to create who we are and who we become—*if* we can learn to understand that even bad experiences can instruct us. Then we can discipline ourselves to realize that no matter what it is we experience, "this too shall pass."[17] With this understanding, we can proceed along our life journey better equipped for growth and development and be insulated from unnecessary emotional overreaction. In the words of Neale Donald Walsch in *Conversations with God*, "You can choose to be a person who has resulted simply from what has happened, or from what you have chosen to be and do about what has happened. It is in the latter form that creation of Self becomes conscious. It is on the second expression that Self becomes realized." As I have taught my children since they were very young, "It is not what happens to me that matters; all that matters is how I *deal* with what happens to me."[18]

If someone you have opened yourself up to hurts you, betrays you, or breaks your heart, forgive them, for they have helped you to learn about trust and the importance of being cautious when you open your heart. If someone loves you, love them back unconditionally—not only because they love you, but also because they are teaching you to love and how to open your heart.

We must make every day count by embracing the people and circumstances

---

[16] https://en.wikipedia.org/wiki/Helen_Keller

[17] This famous saying will be further discussed in the Appendix, below.

[18] This is a paraphrase of a quote from Epictetus: "It's not what happens to you, but how you react to it that matters."

that cross our paths, regardless of our initial perception of them. We must appreciate every moment, taking from it everything that we possibly can, knowing that ultimately a greater purpose will be served. As Nicholas Evans suggested in *The Horse Whisperer*, each now is but a moment on the trail of all nows.

An untold treasure will unfold if we talk to people to whom we have never talked before, actually listening to what they have to say. As my friend Neil J. Cantor liked to say, "Listen loudly." That is, listen to what people are saying and absorb their words and meanings without formulating your own responses as they are speaking. We must let ourselves fall in love, again and again, and set our sights high. The capacity to love is probably the greatest gift that human beings have. As I wrote in a paper years ago, "Life was not meant to be led like a Shakespearean soliloquy."

When the right love comes along, he or she may be camouflaged and masked in a presentation that we do not expect or are used to. We may eventually realize that everything we went through up until then served to enable us to contribute to a greater love than we ever thought possible. All relationships are sacred since they provide us with life's grandest opportunities. Yet, the chance to experience and be a contributing part of a very special relationship between two people is life's most precious gift and blessing.

I am not the person I was before now, nor will I ever be. You are not the person you were before now, nor will you ever be. No matter what the circumstances were or could have been, we must evolve. We must go forward, carrying with us the events, positive or negative, that were—realizing, however, that in fact they *were*, not *are*.

Life has a longing for itself. It must proliferate, even in the face-of tragedy. Perhaps it will take a form that is different—shaped, if you will, by the imposed constraints of the situations that just occurred.

We are the architects of our own lives. We can make them anything we wish. Things and people have a way of rising to the level of the expectations we place on them. If we can learn to discipline ourselves to maintain our attitudes at the same level while we are waiting for our expectations to become reality, our journeys will be less disappointing, and the chances of our expectations actually coming to fruition will be greater.

The following note was originally written in 1998, and then updated as shown below in 2018.

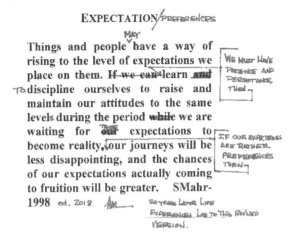

Things and people have a way of rising to the level of expectations we place on them. ~~If we can~~ learn ~~and~~ discipline ourselves to raise and maintain our attitudes to the same levels during the period ~~while~~ we are waiting for ~~our~~ expectations to become reality, our journeys will be less disappointing, and the chances of our expectations actually coming to fruition will be greater. SMahr-1998 ed. 2018

Figure 1: Expectations and Preferences

Do you know your "WHY"?

Knowing your WHY can help you to understand your purpose.

Simon Sinek has written: "Once you understand your WHY, you'll be able to clearly articulate what makes you feel fulfilled and to better understand what drives your behavior when you're at your natural best. When you can do that, you'll have a point of reference for everything you do going forward. You'll be able to make more intentional choices in your life."[19]

Assess yourself by asking these basic questions:

1. What is it (may be multiple things) that gives you joy and makes you feel passionate?
2. What strengths do you have within you that come naturally to you?
3. How do you assess your life?
4. How do you take accountability for that assessment?
5. What activities do you partake in when time seems not to be present?
6. Where and how do you add value not only to your life, but to the lives of others?

---

[19]Simon Sinek, *Find Your Why: A Practical Guide for Finding Purpose for You and Your Team* (New York: Penguin, 2017).

Continually answering these questions will reveal to you your purpose and what direction you should take in your life. By the way, be prepared to change direction as the answers to the questions change.

The purpose of life is a life of purpose.

—Robert Byrne[20]

BE | DO | HAVE
Be — We Are
Do — We Create
Have — We Produce

---

[20]En.wikipedia.org/wiki/Robert_Byrne_(author)/.

CHAPTER 3

ATTITUDE, MINDSET, BELIEFS

Creation is an act of will.

—From the film *Jurassic Park*

I felt somewhat unqualified to contribute to the themes of this chapter when I started to write it initially back in the early 1990s, when my life was going through a low period. On reflection, however, it became apparent that it might be helpful to anyone reading this chapter to learn from my experience that merely knowing the words *good attitudes* and *proper beliefs* is not productive.

Although I am aware of the theories of many great authors, and have been an avid student of them, I was somehow unable, for reasons unknown, to consistently apply to my own life what I knew to be correct. Daniel Goleman, in his book *Emotional Intelligence*, presents a dichotomy between logical intelligence and emotions. We need to understand that, save for a very few of us who possess "Iron Will" (see Chapter 17, below), we must all learn to recognize, understand, and attempt to control the all too powerful effects that our emotions and emotional baggage have over our logical intelligence in virtually every aspect of our lives. Knowing is never enough. Having an "Iron Will" must underscore most of an individual's actions.

To paraphrase Oliver Wendell Holmes, an individual must at times run with the wind, and at other times run against it, but must always commit to running, not merely walking, and certainly never standing still.

Attitudes, mindsets, and beliefs are literally like a transmission that puts an individual's life into gear. Whether individuals go forward or backward is determined largely by their attitudes, mindsets, and beliefs. One glaring difference between a motor vehicle and a human being is that the latter never remains in neutral. I believe that an individual remaining in neutral is contrary to the physical laws of the universe.

There is a concept called "the Theory of Dynamic Rejuvenation," which basically states that everything living, all energy in whatever form, is either growing or dying. There is no constancy in the universe. This theory applies to the primitive cells in our bodies, as well as to our most complex organs. Virtually everything is caught up in the constant state of motion that we know as life. I call this "The Go-Grow-Quo Theory," which means we either go or grow. There is no status quo.

The first step in knowing how to use this concept to our benefit is to be aware of its source. It has been said that there are two types of people: those who believe they can and those who believe they can't. Actually, in my viewpoint, it's about whether they will or won't. In any event, they are both right. Although it is true to say that each of us is a product of our *external* environment, it is more precise to say with certainty that every one of us experiences life based on the state of our *internal* environment.

According to the ancient legend of Pandora's Box, when Pandora opened the forbidden box, thousands of curses were released. One of them, however—hope—remained positive and stood out among all the negativity she released. The story illustrates that no matter what occurs, one should always maintain hope. Hope is an attitude, a belief, a state of mind. It is something that remains available to all of us, notwithstanding the highs and lows of life that we may experience at any one time.

Denis Waitley, a noted motivational speaker, has taught us the concept that everyone wants to be a winner, a champion, but only a very few are willing to invest the time and effort to become one.[21] Winners all have a deep drive and desire to win, which comes not from external sources but a disciplined internal obsession—an attitude that only allows success by carrying within it an "Iron Will" that is not only determined to succeed, but to continually prevail, persist, and achieve (see Chapter 17, below, on Iron Will).

Having the right attitude, mindset, and belief as a transmission for our lives is a basic foundation for living one's life successfully. As is the case with a motor vehicle, however, simply putting it into gear will not make it go.

---

[21]See www.deniswaitley.com/.

To begin with, it must have fuel. An individual's fuel is hard, dedicated, committed work and effort. A winning individual has to be willing to do those things that most others are not willing to do. Operative in this is doing whatever it takes with intention and a sense of urgency—assuming that what is done is ethical.

Eleanor Roosevelt wisely stated, "No one can make you feel inferior without your consent."[22] Elinor Smith observed, "It has long come to my attention that people of accomplishment rarely sat back and let things happen to them; rather, they went out and happened to things."[23] The power of belief, and a strong positive attitude, coupled with a persistent, committed work ethic with focused concentration, must therefore eventually lead to success.

Having the right attitude, mindset, and beliefs can pave the way to whatever it is we want to achieve. Having the wrong attitude, mindset, and beliefs can sabotage all our efforts, hard work, plans, and goals, possibly leading to our ultimate demise. The right attitude, mindset, and beliefs serve like magnets that draw other people and things to them. Conversely, the wrong attitude, mindset, and beliefs repel other people and things.

In closing this chapter, I would like to demonstrate a means of exploring our thought processes and occasional resulting fears, with an exercise showing how to mitigate them.

To start the exercise, write down a list to the best of your recollection of all the thoughts you have had since waking up this morning. Read those thoughts as if you were someone else, since most of the time we get so consumed by our thoughts that we become invested in them as defining us. Doing this exercise will separate you from your thoughts, enabling you to be an observer of them. The technical term for this is metacognition, which is an awareness and understanding of one's own thought processes. When you act as an observer of your own thoughts, you can reframe them as you choose. By reframing thoughts as their observer, you can shape them into something more helpful or useful to you. In essence, you are looking at your thoughts in a different way. You take a step back and consider all aspects of a situation you find yourself in. One example of a thought distortion might be: *I will never reach my goal.* Two possible reframings of that thought might be: *I will never know unless I try*; or *I have already achieved X percent of my goal.*

Many thought distortions find their genesis in fear. How do you move

---

[22]Eleanor Roosevelt, *This Is My Story* (New York: Simon & Shuster,1937).
[23]En.wikipedia.org/wiki/elinor_smith/.

through fear? By breaking through its barriers. Here is one simple way to assist you:

1. Write down your fears.
2. Reframe them.
3. Repeat what you have reframed to yourself over and over.

Fear of failure is higher when you're not working on the problem. If you are taking action, you are less worried about failure because you realize you can influence the outcome.

—James Clear[24]

Figure 2: Believe in Your Self Katrina Wright

---

[24]See https://jamesclear.com/.

CHAPTER 4

SUCCESS

The talent of success is nothing more than doing what you can do well and doing well whatever you do.

—Henry Wadsworth Longfellow

You are only a success at the moment you perform a successful act.

—Phil Jackson, Coach, Chicago Bulls

Being good stands in the way of being GREAT.

—David Foster

Success is never final. Failure is never fatal. Rather it is the courage to continue that counts above all else.

—Winston Churchill

To begin this chapter, I would like to share with you my viewpoint and adopted mantra that to be truly successful, and to stand out even among those who are also successful, you must "always do as you say, and only say as you will do. Furthermore, make certain that you mean exactly what you say you will do, since that needs to be the level-of excellence you adhere to."

There has been so much written about success. There are so many aphorisms about it that a book could literally be filled up, dedicated to nothing else. One aphorism I especially like is by John C. Maxwell: "Success is the continuous journey towards the realization of predetermined, worthwhile goals."[25] Maxwell is speaking to the fundamental precept of starting with a plan. Without a plan, an individual risks aimless wandering. With a plan, and the belief that success is deserved, an individual can travel on a charted course full of meaningful accomplishment and reward.

Also implicit in Maxwell's aphorism is the concept of process. All too often, we fall into the trap of focusing solely on the result of our efforts or desires, without enjoying the process. Many times, we become discouraged and mired down while doing what it takes to achieve our goals. Since success is clearly an ongoing process, how we adapt with patience and perseverance while we go through the various steps involved becomes tantamount to what benefits we derive from our actions.

The mountain will either love you, caress you, and hold you,

or it will spit you out.

—Folklore saying from Taos, New Mexico

Notwithstanding the myriad generalizations that can be derived from the saying above, success becomes a most powerful phenomenon when individuals learn to identify and be comfortable with their own definition-of what their predetermined worthwhile goals are. Every individual is different and unique. All of us have our own purpose in life. We all have within us talents and abilities to accomplish that purpose—and more. However, we must first reflect on and discover what our purpose is. Then we can inventory what our assets are to enlist them in serving our purpose. Only then can we set out in pursuit of accomplishment.

---

[25]*The Success Journey: The Process of Living Your Dreams* (Nashville, TN: Thomas Nelson, 1997).

18

Once we know our purpose and have formulated our goals without being influenced by the expectations, paradigms, or definitions of others, the ongoing process of working toward achievement should become at least as enjoyable as the achievement itself. In fact, for individuals who truly understand, the process usually becomes even more gratifying. Perhaps therein lies one of the major secrets of success.

To reiterate: to be successful and happy, one must enjoy the process, while keeping a desired result clearly in mind.

A person's attitude and demeanor while pursuing any worthwhile endeavor can either add a dimension of strength, clarity, and advantage to its accomplishment or weigh one down by creating inertia and disadvantage. As previously stated, there are two basic conflicting statements that are both correct. If you believe you can, then you can. If you believe you can't, then you can't. It is the validity of this phenomenon that has led me to teach my children that there is no such word as *can't*. If you can't, it is not because you can't, but rather because you are not able to at this time, since you do not choose to do whatever it takes to make it happen. In the movie *Rocky*, the actor who plays Mick, Rocky's coach, replies to Rocky in his gruff way, when Rocky says he can't do something, *"What's can't? There ain't no cant's! There's no cant's. We don't allow no cant's."*

There is a characteristic of success that was demonstrated by the habits of one of the most famous of all biblical personalities, King David. I learned it from a book entitled *Toward a Meaningful Life* by Simon Jacobson.[26] To paraphrase Jacobson, King David always woke up extremely early in the morning. Not only that, but when he woke, "he rose like a lion." Most of us are barely able to pull ourselves out of bed in the morning. But imagine the advantage that King David had as he leaped out of bed like a predator chasing his prey, ready for virtually anything. He greeted each day with an internal fire and euphoria, arming himself with the tools of expectation and certainty of accomplishment. David sought to master and conquer life. His day was literally jump-started with passion and enthusiasm. From the very first moment that he arose, he maintained that same intense level throughout the day with a clearly defined mission. No one and nothing could dissuade him from executing and realizing his objectives. After all, he was certain that he would succeed, and, as history documents, succeed he did. The message-of David's story is clear. The

---

[26]Simon Jacobson, *Toward a Meaningful Life: The Wisdom of the Rebbe* (New York: William Morrow, 1995).

evidence from those who have enjoyed great levels of success in the past is available for each of us to learn from and model after in our own lives.

In my view, the formula for success can be simply stated by two acronyms that I developed and have tried to use in my own life: CAPIP—conceive, analyze, prepare, implement, and produce; and DAPIP—desire, attitude, patience, intent, and persistence.

$$Your\ Life \times [CAPIP + DAPIP] = Success$$

Meir Ezra, a friend of mine who in my view is a "master" coach, teacher, entrepreneur, and international speaker, introduced me to the following concepts:

Success is the sum of all validated improvements.

Success and failure should be greeted with the same level of enthusiasm.

People in general have a tendency to believe that everything happens for a reason. Therefore, they always look for the why. Successful people don't ask why, they create results. They do so by deciding and making what they have decided happen. Looking for reasons why means you are effect, not cause. Being at cause, you don't permit things to happen to you and react. Rather, you create and bring about a result you seek in a proactive manner.

A Paradox of Success: "To expand your success, you must narrow your focus and stay focused."[27]

Using the second concept, above, I posed to Kristmundur Ágúst Jonsson, a very rough draft of the concept in an attempt to describe by a back-of-the-

---

[27]From an online presentation given by Meir Ezra of meirezra.com/.

napkin sketch an illustration showing the results of three possible scenarios of levels of enthusiasm toward success and failure. Kristmundur has a degree in discrete mathematics and computer science and has completed his master's degree in scientific computing and theoretical computer science/artificial intelligence at the KTH Royal Institute of Technology in Stockholm, Sweden. In Figure 2, I share what I presented to him. Then you will see the model he created.

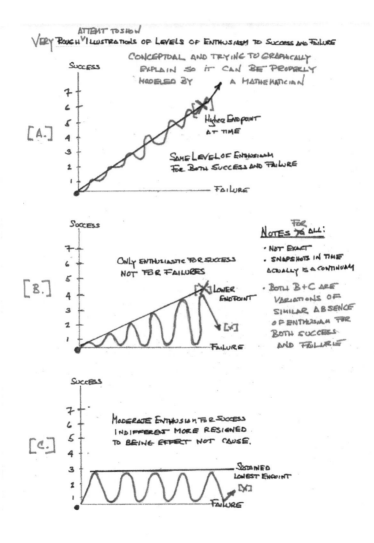

Figure 3: Success and Enthusiasm

Here is an image of the model that Kristmundur Ágúst Jonsson created, using the following equation:

(Amount of enthusiasm while successful) * (Amount of enthusiasm while not successful) = Degree of success

The model has the following properties:

1. Degree of success is minimized when enthusiasm in one or both categories is 0 (e.g., enthusiasm in success or failure).
2. The model is maximized when enthusiasm is highest for both.

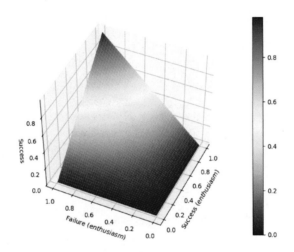

Figure 4: The Kristmundur Model of Success and Enthusiasm
Note: The Actual Model he created was 3D and in video format, the image depicted above is one from what would have required over 7 still images to illustrate

Below is an e-mail I sent to my son when he was 16:

Subj:	**Very Important to do Son**
Date:	5/28/01
To Email:	AJMSTR

Son,
Please print this out where you can see it and read it daily:
In sports, your life, schoolwork, relationships, and everything else you do and/or encounter as you go through your life, you will EXCEL if you do these four things:

1. Focus: Have Commitment
2. Iron Will: Discipline
3. Time Management
4. Practice, Drill, Rehearse, Execute, Repeat

I love you Mucho Grande.
Dad
NOTE: These four things do not come easily though, son. You must *work* on them and be aware of them *all* the time.

To summarize this chapter on success, please consider the following:

Success comes through a Cycle of Improvement (1–5):

1. Have Awareness: Identify what needs improving
2. Be Deliberate: Focus on specific areas to improve
3. Make Incremental Gains: Small regular gains consistently
4. Develop Habits: Practice and the effort becomes automatic
5. Repeat: Begin again

BE | DO | HAVE
Be — We Are
Do — We Create
Have — We Produce

Most people think *incorrectly* that the sequence is not BE | DO | HAVE, but *have | do | be.* In other words, they think: *If I have what I want, then I can do the things I want to do, and then I can be the person I want to be.*

Operating on that false model almost assuredly means that they will struggle and fail most of the time.

The correct model, which results in less struggle and more success is:

BE | DO | HAVE

To reach a goal, BE the person who you want to be as if you already have achieved the goal. Doing so will cause you to DO the things necessary to HAVE exactly what you want to achieve.

Part and parcel of success attainment is problem-solving, or as I like to refer to it, *solution discovery*. The three steps outlined below will serve to eradicate any problem encountered in the physical universe (comprised-of somethings) and result in solutions. First of all, as my friend Meir Ezra shared with me, we must first define what a problem means and agree on its definition. Let's agree to define a problem as one force opposing a counterforce in a way that both exist as a reality. In essence, one side is pushing against the other. When an individual experiences a problem, but then decides to commit to becoming a cause rather than an effect, the pushing stops, the problem dissipates, and the solution appears, since something cannot push against nothing. Something can only push against something.

Steps to Solution Discovery (Ergo Problem-Solving)
1. Name the perceived problem, whatever it may be, and write it down.

2. Invent solutions (come up with ideas) sourced from the spiritual universe (comprised of nothings) and write them down under the problem identified in step 1. The ideas do not need to be practical, and you need not give any consideration to whether or not they are realistic or possible.

3. Continue to create idea after idea as you follow step 2, above. Read to yourself every day what you have written for steps 1 and 2, above. At some point, the problem will suddenly dissipate and no longer exist as part of your reality.

BE | DO | HAVE

CHAPTER 5

BALANCE

We are what we repeatedly do. Excellence then is not an act, but a habit.

—Aristotle

What I dream of is an art of balance, of purity and serenity devoid of troubling or depressing subject matter—a soothing, calming influence on the mind, rather like a good armchair which provides relaxation from physical fatigue.

—Henri Matisse

Just as your car runs more smoothly and requires less energy to go faster and farther when the wheels are in perfect alignment, you perform better when your thoughts, feelings, emotions, goals, and values are in balance.

—Brian Tracy

Balance is perhaps one of the most desired qualities of life, albeit elusive to many. It may also be the single most important element of successful life management. It is an important and conditioned habit that needs continual monitoring and implementing. The various components of life that each of us experiences have inherent demands and require a commitment of time and energy. These areas include self-development, friends, family, romance, career, personal finance, health, fitness, recreation, and spirituality. A balance of all of them is required in order to fully experience the quality of life and ultimate success and happiness in everything we desire.

All of life as we know it is interdependent. Balancing all the various components of our lives optimizes our life experiences. Balancing is an art form. On a personal level, it is perhaps one of the most difficult things to achieve and then maintain. No matter how committed or successful an individual may be in one or more areas of life, that success ultimately intersects with the other areas as well. Attention, time, commitment, and energy must be channeled into each area of life. Although an individual can and should focus more energy and effort into a particular area, that may be lacking at a certain time. Thus, ignoring all other areas of life is not only dangerous but ultimately self-defeating.

Balance has most certainly been mastered by "mother nature." It is the essence of everything that co-exists in the universe. Without balance, there would be chaos and random happenstance. With it, there is order and purpose. In the Disney movie *The Lion King*, Mufasa says, "Everything you see exists together in delicate balance. As king you need to understand that balance and respect all creatures; from the crawling ant to the leaping antelope."

Balance, however, is more than an art form. It is actually a discipline—a never-ending process to be worked toward. To be out of balance is to experience unnecessary highs and lows. If one depends on one's personality and individual characteristics, a certain amount of highs and lows in one's life can be good; in fact, those highs and lows can yield high levels of creativity. Generally, however, a more stable, balanced approach yields a better result.

Envision a seesaw. When one side of the seesaw gets out of balance with the other, it causes its opposite to go either up or down. When both sides are in balance, the seesaw remains level and stable. However, the fun of being on a seesaw does not come from remaining level and straight, but from going up and down. This is also true of life in general, which is once again an example of the art form of balance. Even being in balance to varying degrees requires a type of balance. If one is always at one extreme or the other, one's time is never completely satisfying and fulfilling.

A method of determining the level of balance in one's life, which was first introduced to me years ago by my friend Bonnie Marshall Gorbaty, who learned it as a trainer for the Success Motivational Institute, is called "SMI's Wheel of Life." When I reached out to Bonnie to discuss my inclusion in this book of what she had shared with me many years ago, she added the concept of *Integration*. I asked her if she would write something about it to add to this chapter, and she provided the following:

I have been noticing a pattern over the last three decades in how our lives are being more fully supported through different worlds of information and life experience coming together into one picture. It started back in 1980, when I was introduced to the Success Motivation Institute out of Waco, Texas. SMI presented a concept called "The Wheel of Life," which suggested how one could best manage one's life by looking at all the major aspects of life, then making decisions in each aspect to support, complement, and inspire a whole life. As a management consultant working with small business owners, I would see it play out in the financial sector with a concept called "The Balanced Scorecard," which showcased how all aspects of a business's performance needed to be looked at simultaneously to identify important patterns for company success beyond just the normal Profit & Loss (P&L) and Balance Sheet.

As a yoga teacher and therapist, I learned, explored, and experienced firsthand how the human being is an integrated whole made up of body, mind, and soul. Separating these three critical ingredients makes one susceptible to a range-of illnesses. In the work of Maxwell Maltz called *Psycho-Cybernetics*, he found out firsthand that treating a physical issue (in this case, a surgical facelift) without looking at the underlying mental issue (often related to poor self-esteem or anxiety) created the opposite outcome (a facelift that quickly reverted back).[28]

All of these experiences are examples of the growing trend toward integration. The world is an integrated system made up of other integrated systems with parts that are all working either in balance and harmony or imbalance and disharmony. The evolution of the human experience is to realize this reality and learn how to live a more integrated life in all aspects of our life.

---

[28](New York: Penguin Random House, 2015).

There are wheel-of-life templates that are readily available, and often free, on the internet. Basically, they divide a circle into sections, each of which is an area in one's life. Some of the more popular areas are: self-development, professional and personal growth, business/career, personal finances, health and fitness, recreation, spirituality, romance, family, and life purpose.

If one divides a circle into sections, and each section is an area of your life, then moving upward from the center point of the circle along the radius to the top of the circle, draw a line that shows where that area is in your life (e.g., career). One can easily see which areas need more attention and improvement than others. The object, of course, would be to have as close to complete balance as possible in all the areas, as would be indicated by an equidistant circumference.

Figure 5: The Success Motivation Institute's Wheel of Life

Individuals who accept life as a spectator activity are in a state of imbalance. The participants in life, the players, are the ones who create a balanced existence. Clearly, the key to a sustained, productive, happy, and successful life is to develop and master the habit of balance, and then to learn how to monitor and maintain it. Balance, of course, like other things that we have discussed and will discuss in this book, is subject to constant change. For example, when we buy a new car, we have perfectly balanced new tires and a smooth riding vehicle. As we put more miles on the car, the tires wear out, going out of balance, and the ride is not as smooth anymore. So, we buy new tires, get them balanced, and once again we have a smooth ride. So it is with our lives as we transition and evolve. Balance in our lives is a moving target that we must continually and consciously work toward having. As Wayne Dyer observes in *Being in Balance*, "Getting in balance is not so much about adopting new strategies to change your behaviors, as it is about realigning yourself in all of your thoughts so as to create a balance between what you desire and how you conduct your life on a daily basis."[29]

Figure 6: All We Have is Now Mikael Cho

---

[29]Wayne Dyer, *Being in Balance*, available at https://www.hayhouse.com/.

CHAPTER 6

ORGANIZATION AND TIME MANAGEMENT

The key to time management is to see the value of every moment.... The realization of this enables you to see that there are millions of moments on the path to any worthwhile achievement. You cannot add more minutes to the day, but you can utilize each one to the fullest. This can be done by totally investing yourself in the one activity you are engaged in at any moment. Concentrate at that moment, ignoring everything that came before it and after it.

—Simon Jacobson

Plan your work for today and then work your plan. Do it now, because today will become tomorrow very, very soon.

—Norman Vincent Peale

Realize there is a high probability of low probability events occurring. There is always a situation, it could become a crisis or simply a matter of handling an issue.

—Marshall Goldsmith

Have you ever heard a rationalization that sounds like this? "If only I had the time. I just can't seem to find the time. I'm just too busy. I know I could do it. If only I had time, but I don't. I'm working a full-time job. I even have to make time to be with my family. There's no time for anything."

These sentiments, among others, are merely excuses for lacking an organized program to plan and make maximum effective use of time. Malcolm X said, "In all of our deeds, the proper value and respect for time determines our success or failure."[30] Time is an asset, not a liability. If we learn to work effectively with the time we are allotted, and not become intimidated or overwhelmed by it, we can learn to focus and use time as our ally, rather than seeing it as our adversary. Did you ever hear the old adage, "If you want to get something done, give it to a busy successful person?" Why is that so? Because busy, successful people recognize the power of being organized and managing their time properly. They always find the time to make things happen, no matter how busy they are. It's a matter of priority and focused productivity. Maintaining success is not accidental. Rather, it comes from effectively working proven formulas. Organization and time management are among the most fundamental ingredients of those formulas.

Time management is the ability to plan and control how you spend the hours in a day, week, month, or year to effectively accomplish your *goals*.

To successfully manage time and gain optimal results, you must organize your professional and personal tasks, based on how urgent and important they are, taking care of the most urgent and important first, followed by activities that are not urgent, but still important. By prioritizing, you can focus your time and energy where they matter most.

Figure 6, below, shows the Eisenhower Matrix,[31] a popular time-management strategy for assessing and prioritizing tasks. Each quadrant has examples for types of activities and the order in which to handle them.

---

[30]https://www.goodreads.com/quotes/930133-in-all-our-deeds-the-proper-value-and-respect-for/.

[31]Dwight D. Eisenhower was the 34th president of the United States, from 1953 to 1961. Before becoming president, he served as a general in the United States Army and as the Allied Forces Supreme Commander during World War II. He also later became NATO's first supreme commander. Eisenhower had to continuously make tough decisions about which of the many tasks he should focus on each day. That finally led him to invent the world-famous Eisenhower principle, which today helps us to prioritize by urgency and importance.

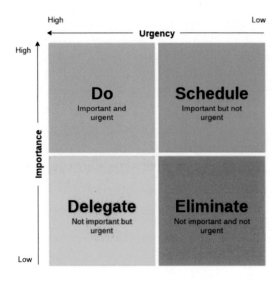

Figure 7: The Eisenhower Matrix

To paraphrase a metaphor used by Tom Hopkins[32]:

> Imagine if you will that you do your banking with a particular bank that credits your bank account each morning with $86,400.00. At the end of each twenty-four-hour period, this bank zero-balances your account, canceling out whatever part of the initial deposit you failed to use during the day. What would you do? Would you attempt to use all that has been allotted to you, or give up some of it as lost, never to be replaced? There is such a bank for each of us. However, rather than deposit dollars into our accounts, it deposits seconds. Its name is time. Each morning, it credits each of us with 86,400 seconds. There are no balances carried over to the next day. Whatever we didn't use during that day is lost forever. A new deposit, however, is made the next day and every day thereafter with exactly the same amount. Each day is a new day. Each

[32]Tomhopkins.com/.

day we get to choose how much of our daily allocation we will use, and how much will be wasted. The question we each ask is, How much of our precious irreplaceable account balance are we willing to lose?

Before answering this question, we must determine whether we desire ultimate success or failure. The choice is ours. How will we use our time? Will we maximize it effectively or squander it inefficiently? As I previously stated, I am convinced that if we choose to focus, remain organized, and remain committed to getting the most out of what time gives us each day, we will ultimately be successful, because we are committed to action and not inaction, balance and not imbalance. The byproduct of this commitment is that we will have ample time for whatever we desire.

We all have the same twenty-four hours in a day, every day. It is what we choose to *do* with our twenty-four hours, and how we choose to *manage* our time, that ultimately determine our successes. We must always ask the question, Am I doing the most productive thing possible at any given moment?

Even relaxing or partying can be the most productive activity possible, if that is what you have planned to do at the time. It is of paramount importance in organizing oneself to not confuse activity with accomplishment. The measure, rather, is to always look for results. Focus. Focus. Focus.

Imagine this. Despite your very busy schedule, you are offered a key to a locker in a bus terminal in Los Angeles, California, which contains a combination to a safe in New York City. In that safe, there is a cashier's check made payable to you for one million dollars, with an endorsement restriction on it that it can only be cashed when you show proof that you drove by car from your home in Los Angeles, picked up the combination and directions to the safe, and then drove directly to New York to pick up the check. On the way there, you must stop three times each day to interact with random individuals, have your photo taken with them, and view and experience something specific to the area in which you meet them. Then, when you arrive in New York, and show the documentation of your activities, the money is yours. Would you do it? If you knew with absolute certainty that the money would be yours if you did all this, could you find the time to do it?[33]

The answer should be obvious, so therefore there really is no such thing as not enough time. It is all just a matter of priorities and balance. There really is time for anything that you want and choose to make the time for. Where there is a will, there is a way. A while ago, I was in my chiropractor's office, having a conversation with his assistant. As I joked with her about not complying with the frequency of the treatments I was receiving, I said, "Well, I guess the old saying, 'You can lead a horse to water, but you can't make it drink,' is true."

She replied, "No, it isn't. You can make it drink if you put enough salt in its food."

Doing things most efficiently and effectively can be accomplished with cycles of action. The conventional wisdom is that a cycle of action is not a linear process that begins and ends, but rather a series of thoughtful, purposeful steps undertaken to refine and focus an action plan, make progress toward goals, review what is working and what is not, and adjust priorities in response to emerging needs.

My belief, as first introduced to me by Ken Kaufman, is that a cycle-of action *can* in fact be a linear process that begins and ends. It can be a process of: START: CHANGE: STOP.[34]

That, then, is a *closed* cycle of action. In one's day-to-day activities, achievement and optimizing time management can best be achieved by greeting tasks and doing them as they present. Hence, the *do it now* reference.

If one permits too many *open* cycles of action, one's "to do list' becomes increasingly vast, and many of one's tasks are left undone. Disorganization becomes normative, and then there is never enough time.

Closed cycles of action reduce clutter and stress, removing the sense-of being overwhelmed. Closed cycles of action produce the space to continue to create. In essence, mastering this art reinforces that you are a cause and not an effect.

---

[33]I first heard this idea at a seminar with my dear friend Richard Gorbaty.

[34]The signature line at the end of my e-mails is: "Always Go Great | START : CHANGE: STOP."

Closed cycles of action create time!

Time Managed *minus* Time Spent = Timing

It is of tantamount importance to be keenly aware of not permitting closed cycles of action to rush your decision-making merely for the sake of completing the cycle. All pertinent data and clear processing of them must first be weighed and evaluated.

Time becomes one of the most valuable commodities as we get older. Although no individuals truly know how much time they have left in this physical existence, as they add on years they become aware, to paraphrase Anthony Hopkins, that they have more days behind them than they have ahead. However, that should not give them license to lament how much time in life they have left; rather, they should maximize every moment and live whatever time remains to the fullest.

In the television series *Blacklist*, James Spader's character, Raymond Reddington, says in one episode:

[I am] on a sailboat, surrounded by sea with no land in sight, without even the possibility of sighting land for days to come. To stand at the helm of your own destiny. I want that, one more time. I want to be in the Piazza del Campo in Siena to feel the surge as ten racehorses go thundering by. I want another meal in Paris, at L'Ambroisie. At the Place des Vosges, I want another bottle of wine. And then another. I want the warmth of a woman and a cool set of sheets. One more night of jazz at the Vanguard. I want to stand on the summits and smoke Cubans and feel the sun on my face for as long as I can. Walk on the wall again. Climb the tower. Ride the river. Stare at the frescos. I want to sit in the garden and read one more good book. Most of all, I want to sleep. I want to sleep like I slept when I was a boy. Give me that, just one time, and that… that's why I won't allow that punk out there to get the best of me, let alone the last of me.

Use your time wisely and efficiently to experience what you want, substituting your desires for your version of Raymond Reddington's.

Live your life with purpose.

> *It should not be enough to have lived. We should be determined to live for something.*

> —Winston Churchill

Live your life happily.

> *There is no path to happiness. Happiness is the path.*

> —Buddha

Maintain frequent contact and interaction with family and friends that you love.

> *There is nothing on this Earth to be prized more than true friendship.*

> —Thomas Aquinas

Don't waste time and energy on begrudging others or seeking revenge.

> *Holding onto a grudge is like swallowing poison and expecting the other person to die."*

> —Buddha

Recognize your passions and use your time in their pursuit.

> *Always remember, you have within you the strength, the patience, and the passion to reach for the stars to change the world.*

> —Harriet Tubman

> *I have to face life with a newly found passion. I must rediscover the irresistible will to learn, to live, and to love.*

> —Andrea Bocelli

CHAPTER 7

MARKETING: PACKAGING AND PRESENTING YOURSELF IN EVERYTHING YOU DO

Wow, you look so beautiful. That is not just a dress, it is a scene from an Audrey Hepburn movie.

—Tom Cruise in the movie *Jerry McGuire*

Perhaps how we appear to others, both in first impressions and thereafter, is one of the easiest things for us to control, and yet one of the most powerful tools that we have available to us. How we present ourselves to others silently advocates for us in everything we do or undertake. In Carlos Castaneda's *The Teachings of Don Juan*, Don Juan says, "A good leaving is just as important as a good arriving."[35]

To help understand the importance of self-marketing and presenting yourself in everything you do professionally or personally, you must first agree that it is in essence always an aspect of sales. So with that as a scenario, all the world truly becomes a stage, and we then become sales representatives, playing to the hardest audience of all, our customers. I use the word *customers* loosely. However, the concept applies to our family members, friends, mates, lovers, etc.

We have all heard the adage, "Never judge a book by its cover." However, most of us are attracted to books that have interesting covers. That is not to say that substance is not of paramount importance, but what attracts us or draws us initially is the scope, packaging, and presentation of everything we encounter.

To be successful in interpersonal relations, whether in social, family, or business activities, how we appear is the first step in our general acceptance.

---

[35]New York: Washington Square Press, 1968.

Therefore, it is incumbent upon us to back up what it is we present with substance, based on actions and performance. As in most things, there is a delicate balance that must be maintained to avoid getting caught up in having too much "form over substance" in one's life.

First impressions are important, not only for others, but for us as well. How others perceive us sets the standard for how they will accept us and interact with us. It also impacts how *we* act. Preparation then becomes a highly important aspect of how we live our lives. If we prepare adequately, we will have ample opportunity to make sure that the way we present ourselves is received in the most favorable terms. Adequate preparation enables us to gain an edge in what is to follow. Presentations can speak without sounds.

How we look conveys how we feel and how successful we appear to be. We all have mental pictures of ourselves, or self-images. Creating a powerful self-image through how we package ourselves allows us to carry a certain air about us that portrays success and confidence. Both are powerful magnets that attract others to us, like moths to a light.

Leonardo DaVinci said, "All of our knowledge and our emotional responses have their origins in our perceptions." How we package and present ourselves is also a type of proactive approach that enables us to convey to others the image and persona we desire and want to create. In the twelve steps of Alcoholics Anonymous, members are taught to "fake it until you make it." Our packaging enables us to achieve what we want to become. The starting point is to look the part, which then leads to becoming what we are trying to create within ourselves. We must, however, always keep in mind that while creating whatever image we desire, our obligation in this life is to be true to ourselves. We must not just become; we must be. Dare to be great, and the chances are that you *will* be great.

WANT AMAZING?

THEN BE AMAZING

CHAPTER 8

BUSINESS AND CAREER

It is neither wealth nor splendor, but tranquility and occupation, that gives

happiness.

—Thomas Jefferson, *Wealth and Poverty*

As first introduced to me by Ken Kaufman, "Production is the basis for morale." In other words, to optimize our productivity, it helps to be happy and to enjoy what we are doing while we are producing. Perhaps that may seem a bit contradictory. What comes first? To be ultimately successful, to realize one's full potential, the key lies in truly enjoying the process of production. When we are able to enjoy what we are doing, we synchronize with our efforts, and our levels of concentration and attention to the tasks at hand become so much more intense and thereby effective. Our labor becomes a natural expression of our inner desires. We become productive. We become the process of productivity. When we are happy, more often than not we become highly successful. Work seems to be effortless. Our productivity and performance are enhanced to higher levels than we ever planned on.

Sigmund Freud said, when he was once asked about how to achieve happiness, "Simply work and love." We all have special talents—skills or latent abilities; callings, if you will—to identify and then to utilize in our business, career, or vocation. The art is to discover what those talents are and then to use them.

There is a parable about a frog and a scorpion meeting at a river at the edge of a forest that is burning down. The scorpion is in front of the frog, blocking his way to the river. There is no way to safety for the frog except to go across the river to the other side. Of course, the frog can swim across, but the scorpion is blocking his way with its lethal stinger. On the other hand, the scorpion cannot swim and is faced with the dilemma of negotiating with the frog to get across. The scorpion proposes that if the frog lets the scorpion get on his back as the frog swims to safety, they will both survive. The frog is skeptical and asks what assurance he has that the scorpion will not kill him once he lets him on his back. The scorpion says, "Because if I do, we will both drown and surely die." So, the frog lets the scorpion get on his back and starts to swim across. Halfway across the river, the scorpion stings the frog. As the poison starts to work, and they both start to drown, the frog asks, "Why did you do that? Now we will surely both die." The scorpion replies, "Because I am a scorpion, and that is what scorpions do—kill frogs."

We must discover what it is that each one of us does, and then do it— unless, as with the scorpion, it is self-destructive. The results will not only help to pave the way for achieving success, but for realizing happiness and high levels of morale as well. As Anthony Robbins advises, we need to become passionate about what we do. Without passion, we stack the odds against us for realizing optimal experiences in the business career aspect-of our lives.

In his book *Flow*, Mihaly Csikszentmihalyi writes of achieving optimal experience by presenting examples of how life can be made more enjoyable. "Being in flow," he states, "is the way people describe the state of mind when their consciousness is harmoniously ordered, and they want to pursue whatever they are doing for its own sake."[36]

It is a known fact that when a professional athlete is "on his game," he is achieving his peak level of performance. This is also called "being in the zone," which is a state of being where one *is* the doing. Wow! To become the doing! That is something we should each strive for in whatever our chosen course of endeavor is. We optimize our lives and our life's work when we transition them from ordinary into flow-producing activities.

It should be noted, however, that it is generally not possible to remain in the zone at all times. Most of the time, it is possible to be in the field that is

---

[36]New York: HarperCollins, 1991.

right for each of us, but not *all* of the time. Even Michael Jordan,[37] who many believe is one of the greatest of all basketball players, was not in the zone at all times. More often than not, however, he seemed to be able to turn on his zone at key times, and the percentages of optimal performance were stacked heavily in his favor as a result.

How we each choose to frame our work experiences can make what we do either boring, mundane tasks, or exciting, enjoyable, and productive odysseys. Then we can live with a sense of mastery over our work efforts. In whatever we do, however, we must know that, as Vince Lombardi said, "the quality of a person's life is in direct proportion to their commitment to excellence, regardless of their chosen field of endeavor."

I thought it would be appropriate to close this chapter by citing a list of ten principles from an early internal memo at Nike long before the company grew into a global brand. This list is rumored to have been written in 1977 by the first head of marketing, Rob Strasser, and was shared decades later by lead designer Markus Kittner:

1. Our business is change.

2. We're on offense. All the time.

3. Perfect results count—not a perfect process. Break the rules.

4. This is as much about battle as about business.

5. Assume nothing. Make sure people keep their promises. Push yourselves, push others. Stretch the possible.

6. Live off the land.

7. Your job isn't done until *the* job is done.

8. Dangers:
   • Bureaucracy
   • Personal ambition
   • Energy takers vs. energy givers

---

[37]See http://en.wikipedia.org/wiki/Michael_Jordan/.

- Knowing our weaknesses
- Don't get too many things on the platter

9. It won't be pretty.

10. If we do the right things, we'll make money damn near automatic.[38]

Part and parcel of being in business, of having a successful career, profession, vocation, or avocation, regardless of size or scope, is to embrace change. In other words, you must "pivot," or you will simply get left behind. Some of the possible reasons for embracing change include:

- The entire socio-economic world is in a constant state of change.
- Our clients or customers (which comprise our market) need or desire change.
- Technology not only changes but exponentially expands.
- The economy often changes with the changing political climate.
- Individuals change (e.g., by age, interests, skills, needs, etc.)

Figure 8: Change

---

[38]*Principles—For Collective Understanding, Focus and Orchestration.* Some employees claim that Nike founder Phil Knight wrote the list.

Chapter 9

Prioritizing

_____

Twenty years from now you will be more disappointed by the things that you didn't do than by the ones you did do. So throw off the bowlines. Sail away from the safe harbor. Catch the trade winds in your sails. Explore. Dream. Discover.

—Mark Twain

pri·or·i·tize /prī'ôrə͵tīz/
    verb
    gerund or present participle: *prioritizing*
    designate or treat (something) as more important than
        other things. ("prioritize your credit card debt")
    determine the order for dealing with (a series of items
        or tasks) according to their relative importance.
        ("age affects the way people prioritize their goals")[39]

Time is a precious commodity. Unfortunately, many of us do not become aware of this until later in our lives—say, our 30s and beyond. It is then that we suddenly experience the passage of time at such a seemingly rapid pace that it is shocking.

Many of us spend much of our youth addicted to the drama of other people's lives—celebrities and the like. We do so without realizing that the diminishing supply of the time our lives are allocated should dictate that we try to fully experience living our own lives as a priority.

_____

[39]Definitions from Oxford Languages. Https://languages.oup.com/google-dictionary-en/.

To prioritize is to assign levels of importance to tasks, things, people, events, projects, and circumstances throughout the course of our day-to-day activities.

For example, the German people are generally held to be exceptional engineers and scientists. They are reputed to be precision-oriented and highly efficient. Many busy and active people who are accomplished in many arenas of life continuously embrace and understand the importance of prioritizing— at least in a clinical sense. To prioritize is to establish a sense of order in an otherwise chaotic existence.

Random selection yields random results. Selective actions based on a system of prioritizing yield decisive and calculated results. They enable a sequence of actions and a plan for our time and energy, which allows those who use them wisely to do more in less time and more effectively. Prioritizing takes what is most important to each of us among our current tasks or responsibilities, and thereby creates a higher level of accomplishment. The process of prioritization does so by giving the most time and attention to other people and things to which we have commitments.

Each of us should continually assess our priorities and continually refine them to make sure that we have them properly sequenced for our own lives. Of paramount importance, as previously discussed in the chapter on Balance, is understanding the key areas of our lives and prioritizing our actions and our attention to them. Some of these areas of our lives are:

Family
Friends
Health/Fitness/Nutrition
Business/Career
Personal Finances
Self-Development
Romance
Spirituality
Leisure

The art is to discover and maintain balance in all areas of our lives. Yet, there are certain things that require a greater degree of time and attention than others. Of course, these are moving targets and, as such, are subject to change. Priorities change in general, based on the level of importance that we choose to assign to them. Establishing priorities in how we live our lives enables us to live more meaningful, responsible lives, while recognizing that there are always people, circumstances, and things that deserve being prioritized over others.

One method of prioritizing is to create a simple worksheet for the day or week, broken up into three main categories: (1) Must Do; (2) Should Do; and (3) Could Do. Obviously, the Must Do's take precedence over the Should Do's, which in turn take precedence over the Could Do's. Then, to each category, assign a rank of 1 to 5, with 5 being the highest and 1 the lowest.

Must Do	Rank 1–5	Should Do	Rank 1–5	Could Do	Rank 1–5

Figure 9: Prioritizing Chart

Make Certain Not to Lose What You Have for What You Want

It is important to always maintain a safety net or cushion, if you will. This is most important when you have already accomplished things, have things, and your life is going well. There are many people who were successful until they lost almost everything while pursuing greater financial gains in areas outside their primary discipline.

Athletic individuals often injure themselves while pursuing excessive fitness goals.

Productive people become ineffective by ignoring their bandwidth and taking on more projects than they have the capacity to handle effectively.

The key to not losing what you already have in pursuit of what you don't have is to safeguard what you have, build a safe-harbor reserve, moderate your further efforts, and learn the importance of focusing, not spraying.

Action expresses priorities.

—Mahatma Gandhi

Most of us spend too much time on what is urgent and not enough time on what is important.

—Stephen R. Covey

BE | DO | HAVE
Be — We Are
Do — We Create
Have — We Produce

CHAPTER 10

G-SQUARED

Pay Yourself First
Save Save Save

Figure 10: GSquared

It's not now much money you make, but how much money you keep, how hard it works for you, and how many generations you keep it for.

—Robert T. Kiyosaki [40]

G Squared is a saying I came up with that was inspired from an age-old concept. Although I named it GSquared, it was derived from an old Yiddish expression, *Gnavish Gelt*,[41] which means "hidden

---

[40]*Rich Dad Poor Dad* (New York: Warner Books, 1997).

or stolen money." In this case, *stolen* doesn't mean that the money is actually taken illegally; rather, it is put aside from one's daily use and saved for later.

In essence, GSquared refers to various tricks and techniques that can be used to accumulate vast amounts of cash, which, if done properly, can serve as a safety net in extreme emergencies—or maybe even serve as a mechanism to enable you to experience things more fully as your life journey continues.

The Basics of GSquared

Pay yourself first. That is to say, for every dollar that comes into your life, take some off the top and, before funding IRAs or retirement funds, paying bills, traveling, or buying other things, put some away in a separate untouchable cash account.

I use the concept of 80/20. In other words, for every dollar that comes in, I take 80 cents to pay my expenses, and 20 cents I pay to myself and put it away. If 20% is hard for you, start with 10% and make the rule 90/10. Accumulate a liquid money base. Even though it may be low-yielding, never touch it. Instead, build, build, build. Set a goal: $100,000, $250,000, $500,000, $1,000,000, or more in cash. Build your fund until you have achieved your goal, then reassess.

Cash does not mean cash on hand, although I believe you should always have some of that, too. Rather, place liquid cash in some savings vehicle, separate from your normal checking or operating accounts. NOTE: Be mindful of FDIC insurance limits,[42] and make sure your cash accounts are properly safeguarded in whatever institute they are held in.

Don't buy impulsively. Ask yourself if you really need what you are about to buy. I am not suggesting that you deprive yourself. If you can buy something comparable and less expensive, do so, or don't buy it in the first place. If it is less expensive, take the portion of the more expensive thing you were thinking of buying and GSquare the difference, or possibly all of it.

For example, here are some of the tricks I have employed during my life.

---

[41]This expression was taught to me by my mother, who in turn learned it from her mother, and her mother from hers. I started practicing it as a young child, since I had to figure out ways to keep some of the money I earned from mowing lawns, snowplowing driveways, disc jockeying, playing in a band, bagging in a grocery store, working in a drugstore, etc., because all the money I earned had to help pay for family expenses.

[42]As of this writing, those limits are at $250,000 per bank. However, double-check, since the regulations change from time to time. There are different types of insurance for money markets, credit unions, etc.

Let's say you want to buy something that costs $100, when you could buy something adequate for $39.00. By buying the less expensive item, you GSquare the difference of $61.00 into a separate account.

When you get a rebate, or come into extra money, don't commingle it with your normal accounts or cash. GSquare it.

Take advantage of discounts, coupons, and sales, and GSquare the amounts you would have otherwise spent.

If you go out to socialize with others and you pay the bill with your credit card—which, by the way, you should pay when the statement comes due—and your companions give you cash for their portion, take the cash and GSquare it.

When you travel, take an envelope with you. When you go out during your trip, and you are enjoying yourself, instead of ordering that extra appetizer or extra drink, make note of the amount you would have spent and put it in the envelope when you get back to your hotel. You will come back from every trip with extra cash for your GSquared Account, without compromising a good time.

When you receive any refunds, insurance rebates, or other forms of money inflow, GSquare it. GSquare any monetary gifts that you didn't expect.

Become creative with all the ways you can hide or save money that you would otherwise spend and never think about. There are so many examples, and I am sure you can come up with some of your own. The techniques you employ to GSquare are not designed to deprive yourself. Rather, they are designed to provide for yourself and those you love.

Make GSquaring a habit. Do it with a sense of urgency. *Never* allow yourself to delay GSquaring when money in any form comes into your life.

Make a Monthly Budget and Make GSquaring an Integral Part of It

What follows below is excerpted and in some instances paraphrased from other sources on the subject, including Wikihow.[43]

Paying Yourself First Is a Basic Money Habit That Can Create Wealth

According to certified financial planner David Blaylock, CFP, "Paying

---

[43]Available at http://www.wikihow.com/Main-Page/.

yourself first means saving before you do anything else. Try and set aside a certain portion of your income the day you get paid *before* you spend any discretionary money. Most people wait and only save what's left over—that's paying yourself last."[44]

The problem is that by the time you have paid for everything else—rent, groceries, utilities, and maybe even a few dinners out—you often don't have enough left to add to savings—at least, not until your next paycheck. And so the cycle goes.

Paying Yourself First

Decide how much to pay yourself. Experts recommend differing amounts. In the famous personal finance book *The Wealthy Barber*, David Chilton recommends paying yourself 10 to 20 percent of your net or take-home income.[45]

Set a savings goal. Create an account that is separate from all your other accounts. Put money into the account as soon as it is available. The point is to do this *before* you spend money on anything else, including bills and rent.

Leave the money alone. Don't touch it. Don't pull money out of it. You should have a separate fund just for emergencies.

Building savings is an exponentially powerful tool. Its growth may start like a small snowball, but as it rolls downhill, it gains momentum to become much larger. This has often been referred to as the "snowball effect," which is a metaphor for a process that starts out small, but quickly begins to gain momentum, mass, and weight, moving more quickly as it grows. Roll a snowball down a hill, and by the time it reaches the bottom, it will be the size of a boulder.

Most people prioritize spending their money in the following order: bills, fun, saving. There is usually little left over to put in the bank. But by simply moving saving to the front—saving, bills, fun—you can set the money aside *before* you rationalize reasons to spend it.

No one ever says, "Saving was a mistake." No matter your age, begin saving *now*. And if you already save, consider increasing how much you set aside each month.

---

[44]Available at http://www.forbes.com/sites/learnvest/2014/07/24/are-you-paying-yourself-first-the-money-habit-that-can-boost-wealth/#c9eb447732ca/.

[45]David Chilton, *The Wealthy Barber* (Roseville, CA: Prima Publishing, 1998).

Most people can save at least 10 to 20 percent of their income. Although the authors of many personal finance books briefly explore the idea of paying yourself first, David Bach's 2003 bestseller, *The Automatic Millionaire*, is devoted exclusively to that subject.[46] The entire book is a step-by-step guide to developing the saving habit and making it automatic.

Accumulating money and wealth starts with savings, continues by living within your means, setting baseline cash goals, and thereafter investing wisely (thereby making your money work for you).

In the excellent book, *The Millionaire Next Door*,[47] the authors describe seven common denominators among individuals they studied who accumulated wealth:

1. They live well below their means.
2. They allocate their time, energy, and money efficiently, in ways conducive to building wealth.
3. They believe that financial independence is more important than displaying high social status.
4. Their parents did not provide economic outpatient care.
5. Their adult children are economically self-sufficient.
6. They are proficient in targeting market opportunities.
7. They chose the right occupation for them.

So how about you? Do you recognize yourself in any of the five examples below? If so, are you comfortable with your mindset? According to Rachel Cruze, there are five ways that your mindset affects your money:

1. *Spenders vs. Savers*: Spenders see nothing but possibilities when it comes to money, but a saver's first instinct is to not spend it.
2. *Nerds vs. Free Spirits*: Nerds get excited about telling

their money where to go each month. Free spirits are where

---

[46](New York: Crown, 2003).

[47]Thomas J. Stanley and William D. Danko, *The Millionaire Next Door* (Lanham, MD: Taylor Trade Publishing, 1996).

the party is.

3. *Safety vs. Status*: People who value safety want the security that money can bring. Status uses money to measure success.

4. *Abundance vs. Scarcity*: People with an abundance mindset believe there is more than enough money, but those with a scarcity mindset believe money is finite.

5. *Your Family and Childhood*: The mindset that was present in the household you grew up in is probably evident in your beliefs today.[48]

You can change your mindset if you so choose by incorporating the basic concept of GSquaring in your life and increase your bottom line by saving, using whatever tricks and techniques you may come up with to do so.

For everything there is a season. There is a time to sow and a time to reap.[49]

—Pete Seeger

[48]Available at https://www.rachelcruze.com/ and further published at www.success.com/.

[49]Available at http://en.wikipedia.org/wiki/Turn!_Turn!_Turn! "Turn! Turn! Turn! (To Everything There Is a Season)" is a song written by Pete Seeger in the late 1950s, which was first recorded in 1959. The lyrics—except for the title, which is repeated throughout the song, and the final two lines—consist of the first eight verses of the third chapter of the biblical Book of Ecclesiastes.

CHAPTER 11

EXIT PLANS – FUTURE THINKING

Wisdom is knowing what to do next; virtue is doing it.

—David Star Jordan[50]

Future Thinking is to think ahead, the definition of the [idiom] "think ahead": to prepare for a future event or situation by thinking about what might happen, i.e., "We should have thought ahead and brought an umbrella."

—Merriam Webster Collegiate Dictionary

It has been said many times that "the best offense is a good defense." Incorporating exit plans into every area of your life will help you to prepare for any eventuality, thereby increasing the possibilities for your realizing whatever ultimate results you desire.

Exit plans are a form of "future thinking"—that is to say, thinking of things that could possibly occur. Before making a move in a game of chess, grandmasters will attempt to think of all the moves and variations that could be a consequence of their move and how their overall game plan might be affected as a result. Utilizing exit plans and strategies mitigates potential downsides that you can experience in life. You have all heard the old saying, "It is better to be safe than sorry." This is a form of exit planning/future

---

[50]*The Philosophy of Despair* (Cambridge, MA: Harvard University Library, 1902).

thinking. By thinking ahead about possible eventualities, you can be better prepared to take advantage of situations and things before they happen.

As you plan out your life, there will always be random occurrences and infinite probabilities that can cause you to suddenly be deterred from the direction you are taking or were expecting. For example, you carry a spare tire in the trunk of your car in case you get a flat tire while driving. A proper exit plan not only includes having a spare tire while on the road of life. You must also assure that you have air in the spare tire and that there are tools in the trunk to change the tire.

Most of us know people who always land on their feet, no matter what they may have gone through. Inevitably, those individuals are prepared for happenstance. They are the type of people who have thought through the possibilities, and have alternative plans to compensate for unseen occurrences. Over the long term, they are more successful than individuals who do not plan ahead. That is actually a key concept of exit plans: *anticipate!*

One definition of luck is that preparation meets opportunity. One of my mentors, Neil J. Cantor, taught me an amended version of that definition: "Luck is when *adequate* preparation meets opportunity." Lucky or successful people are not only prepared for their initial course of action, but they also have exit plans in place before they even start that action. Proper planning and execution of chosen courses of action, with an exit plan in place, alleviates potential disappointment or surprise in everything we do. By always keeping the end in mind, and by thinking of all the possibilities, we in essence safeguard the end result we seek. As has been said, yesterday's preparations, along with today's actions, will determine tomorrow's results.

Exit planning is a skill set that needs to be learned and developed—one that eventually becomes a conditioned automatic reflex and response. You must train yourself to develop exit planning as a focused priority, like professional athletes who train and train for certain moves over and over until those moves become "natural reflexes" in game situations. As a matter-of course, exit planning should become a proactive reflex in all of us, replacing blind response with anticipation. Exit planning/future thinking is not only smart; it serves us as another arrow in our quiver—a resource, so to speak, to help us maintain a smoother course and optimize our life experiences.

CHAPTER 12

HONOR

Honor is simply the morality of superior men.
—H. L. Mencken

If it be a sin to covet honor, I am the most offending soul.
—William Shakespeare, *Henry V*

It is on the beaches of time beyond the reaches of the eradicating waves of cause and effect that people of honor leave their footprints as markers for those of us with aspirations for accomplishment and contributions to society.

Ever since my son was a young boy, I have been teaching him about the importance of being a gentleman. As he got older, he asked me what exactly being a gentleman meant. In response, I developed for him something entitled "A Gentleman's Creed,"[51] which outlines what I think being a gentleman means. The creed begins as follows:

> At all times in every situation and in every circumstance, always be a gentleman. Always ask yourself before taking an action or when interacting with someone or confronted with a situation, "Is what I am about to do or the way I am about to act what a gentleman would do, and/or how can I handle this as

---

[51]See the Appendix, below, for a complete copy of the Gentleman's Creed.

a gentleman should?" A gentleman always acts with honor and according to his own self-imposed code of conduct.

Honor is what permits you to live your life based on standards that, when fully followed, yield satisfaction, success, and respect from ourselves and those with whom we interact.

The Ten Commandments tell us specifically that we should honor our father and mother. All honorable conduct sets the stage for living one's life in an exemplary manner. Honor, integrity, and character are the moral fibers that weave our very existence into an exceptional meaningful experience.

To live honorably, to always act with honor, should be the benchmark-of human conduct in all circumstances. Honor goes beyond the phrase, "My word is my bond." It encompasses striving to always do the right thing. A person who chooses to live honorably in every thought and action stands apart from the masses, just as a beacon from a single lighthouse permeates the darkness of an isolated seacoast. In the process of living honorably, such individuals continually attract other people and things to them—as if they were a magnetic force by virtue of their code of being.

Asian cultures recognize honor as a basic part of their existence. Asians greet each other as "the honorable so and so." They expect honor in all areas of their lives, and they impose a stringent code upon their behavior as a matter of course. "Saving face" is so important to them that some of them even carry it to the extreme of committing suicide, rather than dishonoring their family name.

When I was a boy, my father used to tell me, quoting John Donne, "No man is an island." He would go on to say, "Whatever it is you do or don't do will always have consequences for our entire family, so you should always conduct yourself with honor."

Your honor is the essence of what you really have to offer others as you interact with them and as you live your own life. It is the essence of what you offer yourself as well. The saying goes that you are as weak as your weakest link. Conversely, you are as strong as your strongest link. Honor may very well be your ability to forge the strongest links in the chain that is your life.

The Boy Scout Oath and Law

As an Eagle Scout in the Boy Scouts of America,[52] I learned the Scout

Oath from the very beginning as a Tenderfoot, as the entry-level rank was called. It starts with the word *honor*.

Scout Oath

On my honor I will do my best
to do my duty to God and my country
and to obey the Scout Law.
To help other people at all times.
To keep myself physically strong,
mentally awake, and morally straight.

The Boy Scout Law

A scout is:
Trustworthy,
Loyal,
Helpful,
Friendly,
Courteous,
Kind,
Obedient,
Cheerful,
Thrifty,
Brave,
Clean,
And Reverent

---

[52]Available at https://en.wikipedia.org/wiki/Eagle_Scout_(Boy_Scouts_of_America)/.

CHAPTER 13

LISTENING, AN INTEGRAL PART OF COMMUNICATION

Listen closely and you shall hear.

—Henry Wadsworth Longfellow, "The Ride of Paul Revere"

The single biggest problem of communication is the illusion that it has taken place.

—George Bernard Shaw

Listening is one of the most important parts of communicating. Understanding each word, phrase, or concept that you are listening to is a prerequisite to listening correctly. Listening starts with intention and focus. The goal is to listen actively.

So, what is active listening? It's a way of paying attention. It's fully concentrating on, engaging in, and absorbing what someone else is saying to you. It's displaying obvious and genuine signs, such as eye contact, and it also displays reinforcing responses, such as nodding, agreeing with "yes," and asking related questions for clarification. Active listening is a way to fully hear what people are saying—not just assuming that you know what they are going to say after hearing the first two words and then spending the rest of the time that they are talking preparing a response. Instead, active listening focuses on dropping assumptions and working to understand the feelings, motives, and views of other individuals.

One of the most important aspects of listening is to understand the words or phrases being conveyed by other people. All of the participants in a conversation need to agree about what the others are saying or intending.

People often tend to skip over a word or expression without understanding its meaning or what the user of the word or expression intended as its meaning. The result can then dramatically affect and alter one's understanding of everything else being communicated after that word or expression.

To maximize understanding, the best form of communication is in person, when the participants cannot only listen to *what* is said, but also to *how* it is said (tone, body language, facial expressions, eye positions, etc.).[53]

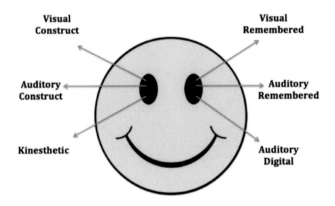

Figure 11: Neurolinguistic Programming (NLP) Eye Cues

Some key *Aspects of Active Listening* are:

> Maintaining eye contact
> Being attentive
> Being open-minded
> Listening to each word or phrase
> Clarifying words or phrases you don't understand
> Visualizing what is being said
> Not interrupting

---

[53]See http://www.nlpu.com/Articles/artic14.htm/.

Asking clarifying questions
Paying attention to nonverbal cues
Summarizing what is said
Obtaining agreement

Throughout the years, communicating in person has become abbreviated, making it less personal and, in many instances, more difficult to gain understanding of the other. For example, instead of in-person face-to-face communication, we started writing letters and making phone calls, and now we are in the age of e-mailing and texting, which by their nature are less exact and often lead to misunderstandings. That was the case even before the introduction of emojis, which have further enhanced the possibilities for misunderstandings.[54]

Listening may be one of the most important skills that we have control over during our lifetimes. Active listening not only includes listening to others, but also listening to the voices that echo within ourselves. Listening is an acquired skill, which improves with practice. It is perhaps the most fundamental and important of all the aspects of communication. The ability to listen well and attentively is the cornerstone of building better interpersonal relationships in all areas of our lives. It might even be argued that good listening may be the single most controllable part of conflict reduction and/or resolution. As my friend and mentor Neil J. Cantor used to say, "Listening is the highest compliment you can give to another, so listen loudly."

Most people never really hear what others are saying to them. As I previously noted, most individuals are busily preparing mentally what they are going to say in response to the little they have already heard. This process causes them to miss out on the rest of what is being said. To fully develop the communication skill of listening, individuals have to learn to discipline themselves to block out distractions, to silence the noise of their thoughts, and to focus all of their attention on what people are saying to them. Good therapists and mental health counselors incorporate this discipline in their work. But the discipline is also utilized by good salespersons, friends, lovers, mates, colleagues, businesspeople, professional service providers, parents, family members, students, and teachers, to name a few. What distracts us and often precludes our ability to listen attentively is our paradigms—that is, our

---

[54]See https://en.wikipedia.org/wiki/Emoji/.

preconceived beliefs. Those paradigms can in turn be further affected by our viewpoints, which in turn are predicated on our data inputs. An important part of life is storytelling. We tell ourselves stories and we've been told stories. What is key is which stories we believe. That reminds me of something my father said to me long ago: "Son, whenever you hear something, always consider the source."

There is an ancient parable that makes this point. Three blind men come across an elephant and attempt to learn what it is, each one touching a different part, but only one part—the trunk, the tusks, or the ears. Therefore, each man comes away with a totally different conception of what an elephant is. The moral of the parable is that humans have a tendency to base absolute truth on their limited subjective experience, ignoring other people's limited subjective experiences, which may be equally true.[55]

A conversation becomes productive when you learn from it rather than just contribute to it. I frequently told my children when they were young and tended to interrupt what was being said to them, "You have two ears, but only one mouth. Use what you have more of." That concept, of course, is well known, but not often practiced. We often hear only what we want to hear. Then, to compound matters, after a time we tend to inaccurately remember what we heard.

There are many factors that can prevent individuals from comprehending what they are listening to. Among those factors are not really wanting to listen, not valuing the person who is speaking, not having any interest in what is being spoken about, not being patient, not having time to listen, and not paying attention because of distractions or desires. Ineffective listening, however, really comes down to a basic lack of priority. Ineffective listening is not only a disservice to the speaker, but also deprives the listener of an opportunity to grow and learn. After all, something can be learned from everyone in every situation.

Listening requires a commitment to individual self-control. Like many of the other skill sets written about in this book, listening requires ongoing practice, drill, and rehearsal, or PDR as Tom Hopkins states in *How to Master the Art of Selling*.[56] Once mastered, however, listening becomes a powerful and highly effective tool.

Understanding what motivates us to listen, based on different situations, is

---

[55]See en.wikipedia.org/wiki/blind_men_and_an_elephant/.
[56](Issaqua, WA: Made for Success Publishing, 1979).

an important step in improving our listening skills. Are we listening for entertainment purposes, inspirational purposes, or motivational purposes? Is our listening intended to seek support or advice? Is our listening out of respect for the speaker or out of an obligation to listen? Is our listening voluntary, or is it required? Each of these listening scenarios and many more can potentially affect the intensity of how we listen to others. A desire to communicate effectively, however, requires us to learn how to listen attentively and effectively in all situations.

When you listen to someone without knowing what the speaker means or what the definition of a certain word, phrase, or sentence is, *stop! Ask!*

All communication must be defined with agreement about the meaning-of what is being communicated. Without that agreement, there is no understanding or effective communication.

Here is a back-of-a-napkin illustration:

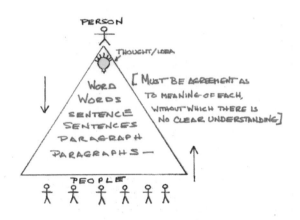

Figure 12: Word-Defining Communication

As of this writing, modern communication through current technological advances, which are of course forever changing, has been compounded by using emojis[57] in texts, e-mails, and instant messages. They are also prevalent in social media such as Facebook, Twitter, LinkedIn, and Instagram. In the

---

[57]See https://en.wikipedia.org/wiki/Emoji/.

shorthand of digital communications, emojis are a visual way of conveying emotion. However, they can be ambiguous and often lead to misunderstandings. The major problem with emojis is their interpretation and meaning. Emojis bring to mind the age-old adage, "A picture is worth a thousand words."

First, it should be noted that different platforms translate and depict emojis differently. Second, emojis often have multiple meanings that not everyone will recognize. Much is being written about the effectiveness of emojis and their potential for misconstruance. Nevertheless, using emojis reinforces what I stated above—namely, that all communication must be defined with agreement and mutual understanding about the intended meaning of what is being communicated. Without that agreement, there can be no understanding or effective communication.

Figure 13: Communications Mia Baker

CHAPTER 14

LEARNING

You are led through your life by the inner learning creature, the playful spiritual being that is your real self. Don't turn away from possible futures before you are certain you don't have anything to learn from them. You are always free to change your mind to choose a different future.... You teach best what you most need to learn.

—Richard Bach, *Illusions*[58]

What is learning? Learning is the process of acquiring new understanding, knowledge, behaviors, skills, values, attitudes, and preferences. The ability to learn is possessed by humans, animals, and some machines. There is also evidence for some kind of learning in certain plants. Some learning is immediate, induced by a single event (e.g., being burned by a hot stove), but much skill and knowledge accumulate from repeated experiences. Changes brought about by learning often last a lifetime.[59]

The subject of learning may seem to be so basic that one may think that everything is already known about it. *Au contraire!* Learning is fundamental to the very existence of life. For example, the process of evolution of organic matter is an innate ability to adapt to environmental changes—a metamorphosis based on new constraints or rules. Adaptation through learning is a metaphor of life's longing for itself.

---

[58](NY: Dell Publishing, Inc., 1977).
[59]See https://en.wikipedia.org/wiki/Learning/.

Many of the characteristics that exist in the human species are explained by evolutionary adaptations that enabled survival. Like all life forms, human beings adapt to their environment. We adapt through variations that increase our ability to survive in a specific environment and its inherent constraints, which disrupt the balance of the previous condition. Examples of environments to which we have adapted include climate, intensity of sunlight, disease, geographic location, altitude, fertility of the ground, temperature, and presence or lack of food and water. One adaptation to the various environments that we occupy is our adaptation to climate, as shown by different skin colorings, which likely were the result over time of the amount of sunlight and ultraviolet radiation to which we were exposed.

Then there are the stressors that derive from sociological changes, such as from agriculture to industry, to current technology, to machine learning and artificial intelligence. Each change and advancement led to new required skills or traits to enable survival.

As Manuj Aggarwal has written:

Technology is progressing rapidly, and it is changing the way we live, work, and play. New inventions are happening, and new paradigms are born almost every day. Conventional concepts we are used to as a human race for decades or even centuries are being disrupted by cutting edge technology.

Even with these universal advantages—we see every individual is slightly different. Some of us can adapt and trust technology much better and faster, while others are slower to embrace these changes. These traits make one person more efficient in the modern world as compared to others. These adaptability traits could affect the quality of life of the individuals and other factors like their financial status and place in the contemporary world. As a result, even a person with a slight physical disadvantage but with robust mental capabilities can flourish in this world.

On the other hand, a lot of the physically demanding obligations have been taken off our plates. We no longer have to hunt for our food. We no longer have to fight off formidable predators on a daily basis. The physical stresses and demands on our bodies have greatly decreased. Machines have taken the intensive work role in industries, agriculture, and transport.[60]

We tend to classify and categorize people, places, and things into "buckets." This is actually an evolutionary psychological adaptation. We compartmentalize our thoughts, ideas, and opinions as we interact with new people, places, and things. Over a long enough period of time, we tend to place into buckets the new experiences we have, in order to reduce any discomfort we have around them. This compartmentalization of adaptation helps us to engage with the environment we are in.

In Chapter 4, I wrote about the Go-Grow-Quo Theory, according to which we either go or grow, or there is no status quo. Learning by definition is an example of that theory. Learning is synonymous with personal growth and development.

Whether we intentionally try to or not, we are always learning. We can maximize the process, however, by a conscious acceptance of learning's importance and by committing ourselves to embracing every opportunity to learn throughout our lives. Learning then becomes a powerful take-charge tool.

From a very young age, my daughter and son shared a daily learning exercise with me. At the end of each day, I would ask them one new thing they had learned that day, and we would then discuss it. As a result of that exercise, we all learned more.

We can learn by *doing*, and we can learn by *not* doing. We can learn by teaching. We can learn by making mistakes. We can learn from our past. We can learn from the pasts of others. We can learn from studying. We can learn from watching. We can learn from experiencing. We can learn from not experiencing. The list could go on and on to fill up this entire book. The important point I am attempting to make here is that learning can best serve us by a proactive rather than a reactive approach. Spectators can learn things,-of course, but it is the players, the participants in the arena of life, who maximize the learning experience and thereby enhance and/or create opportunities.

Throughout life, tragedy strikes all of us at one time or another. Yet, in the midst of the seemingly destructive fire of tragedy lies valuable learning. Somewhere hidden in the smoldering ashes is learning that yields us a base for new growth and development. In the film *Don Juan Demarco*, Marlon Brando's character states, "In the transitional battleground of our adolescence,

---

[60]Available at https://medium.com/@manuj.aggarwal/technological-advances-and-its-effects-on-human-evolution-5329718639e7/.

some of us have surrendered our lives to the momentum of mediocrity. What happened to the celestial fire that used to light our way?"

I suggest that the celestial fire that lights our way is readily available to each and every one of us. We do not have to surrender to mediocrity. Through a dedication to continuous and ongoing learning in everything we do, the celestial fire ignites for each of us, enabling us in turn to illuminate everyone we come into contact with, especially those we cherish and love.

What, then, can we do to be more effective learners? What steps can we each take to dedicate ourselves to be students at all times, open to new data and information that will enable us to share with others and grow within ourselves?

Perhaps, we should begin by accepting the fact that each of us is limited in what we already know and have experienced. The beauty of interacting with others is that there is something to be learned from everyone. The synergistic dynamic of social interaction creates an energy that far exceeds what can be accomplished by individuals acting alone. In fact, that is the underlying premise behind mastermind alliances, which consist of two or more minds working together toward a common objective. The hard part, however, is that we must listen attentively to what others are saying.

To reiterate what was stated in the previous chapter, focused listening to what others are saying without distraction or initial judgments is a form of learning. True listening is the first and one of the most important steps in the learning process. Perhaps, the highest service that one can pay to oneself is to listen to others with focused awareness.

Reading is learning! To read is to avail oneself of the vast treasure that is our birthright. Documentations, observations, experiences, fantasies, theories, creative efforts, beliefs, memories, and discoveries of others are available to each and every one of us through reading, which contains all the accumulated knowledge of the ages. If you really want to learn, become a voracious reader.

When we learn to fully interact with others and our environment, to pass the hurdles and struggles of giving unconditionally, great benefits await us. Windows of new venues for learning and experiencing open for us. The journey of our lives interacting with each other is like circles—sometimes concentric, sometimes overlapping, sometimes separate. How we interpret the lessons our experiences offer us fortifies us to continue our journey, which is never complete. The process remains constant and ongoing—circuitous, if you will. On our own, each of us is never complete. The truest and most beneficial of all life experiences occurs when we learn to connect our individual circle with the circles of others, and thereby the circle of life.

The act of living affords each of us the opportunity to learn lessons. When we do something that fails or turns out badly, that should be construed as a lesson, not a mistake. Our growth is an ongoing process of trial and error. We are intended to learn lessons in life, and we keep experiencing circumstances in various forms until we learn from them. When we finally learn one lesson, we go on to the next. Through every stage, life presents us with learning opportunities. What we make of our lives depends on our choices and ours alone. Within each and every one of us are the tools and resources that are needed.

The following ancient legend was recanted by John Wayne Schlatter in a section entitled "The Magic Pebbles," in his book *Gifts by the Side of the Road*:

> One night, a group of nomads was preparing to retire for the evening, when suddenly they were surrounded by great light. They knew they were in the presence of a celestial being. With great anticipation, they awaited a heavenly message of great importance that they knew must be especially for them.
>
> Finally, the voice spoke, "Gather as many pebbles as you can. Put them in your saddle bags. Travel a day's journey, and tomorrow night will find you glad, and it will find you sad."
>
> After having departed, the nomads shared their disappointment and anger with each other. They had expected the revelation of a great universal truth that would enable them to create wealth, health, and purpose for the world. But instead they were given a menial task that made no sense to them at all. However, the memory of their visitor caused each one to pick up a few pebbles and deposit them in their saddle bags while voicing their displeasure.
>
> They traveled a day's journey, and that night, while making camp, they reached into their saddle bags and discovered every pebble they had gathered had become a diamond. They were glad they had diamonds. They were sad they had not gathered more pebbles.[61]

The experiences of our lives, the people that we come into contact with,

---

[61](Salem, OR: Heart Productions and Publishing, February 2012).

the treasures of the past that await us in literature, art, history, music, and science are all pebbles for each of us to put into our saddle bags. Everything we learn and everyone we learn from is a pebble that will become a diamond. Gather all of the pebbles you can, and delight in the treasure of your diamond collection as you live your life. Adding to each of our collections is a never-ending process. The treasure just grows and grows.

Always
Seek
Knowledge

Figure 14: Unsplash Image

What is your interpretation of the above image?

CHAPTER 15

ELIMINATING NEGATIVITY,
GETTING THINGS DONE EFFICIENTLY,
EXCHANGING IN ABUNDANCE

Figure 15: Glass Empty or Full "When asked if my cup is half-empty or half-full, my only response is that I'm thankful I have a cup" Joseph Greve

It is my intention in this chapter to share in a meaningful way concepts that I have incorporated into my life and deem to be important conditions for one's accomplishments. There is connectivity in the topics selected as parts of a whole, which have interconnecting effects. Some of what follows has been paraphrased from various sources; other thoughts are entirely my own; presented throughout, however, are theories and applied practices that I find instrumental to productive conduct toward a life-of accomplishment in multifaceted venues (e.g., personal, business, career, social, health, fitness, and well-being).

If one agrees with the concept that productivity is one of the bases for morale, and if production is adversely affected by poor time management, which results in lower productivity and therefore lower morale, then having low morale most often leads to negative thinking. Negativity can cause you to languish in a condition of apathy, which in turn reduces your motivation to be productive. You may simply procrastinate or not employ prioritization techniques, and hence remain in a state of inaction. You then dwell on a hill of negativity, becoming a victim of your circumstances. That reduces your ability to address what you can do to make your future different from your past.

Removing negativity from your life requires self-discipline.

One of the most important aspects of building self-discipline is learning how to manage time effectively and efficiently. Productivity and time management are linked and critical to success in more ways than most people realize. Many people have a reasonable understanding of time management, but their productivity is compromised by the problems they experience, most of which are small and repetitive, rather than major events. However, what many people fail to see is that those small repetitive problems compound and thus restrict the quality of the results they achieve.

Time Is a Limited Resource

Lack of available time results from lack of planning, which frequently leads to having to be reactive—always rushing, catching up, or repairing—which in turn yields less effectiveness and productivity.

Management and prioritization of time reduce stress and the resulting negativity that follows.

Better decisions can be made without negativity.

Dealing with others or even with ourselves identifies the modality of exchange we use in our personal and interpersonal relations. There are four types of such exchange.[62] Our gains or losses, wealth or poverty, are largely predicated on our dealings with others or ourselves. Other people, other businesses, other service providers, other family members, our own personal development, the goals we set for ourselves, and so on, are all affected by the four types of exchange that we employ.

---

[62]This concept was introduced to me by Meir Ezra..

Four Types of Exchange Emphasize the Principle of Exchange in Abundance

There are four types of exchange in our personal and interpersonal relations:

1. Criminal Exchange
2. Partial Exchange
3. Fair Exchange
4. Exchange in Abundance

Criminal exchange involves taking something for nothing. There is no real exchange involved. Employees who do not carry out their duties but collect paychecks indulge in criminal exchange. An organization that collects fees for a service or product and never delivers is also committing criminal exchange.

Partial exchange is the act of delivering less than what was agreed upon or expected. This can involve the delivery of only part of a product—as in a flawed product—or a product that is not completely functional. While partial exchange is above criminal exchange, it is not at all acceptable in business or in everyday life.

Fair exchange involves providing a specific product or service, receiving compensation for it, and delivering exactly what one has agreed upon. Most businesses and people operate on the basis of fair exchange.

Exchange in abundance is the highest form of exchange. It does not involve undercharging for a product or service or giving them away. Rather, it involves delivering something more valuable than the recipient expected.

Exchange involves trading valuables for valuables. In life, exchange occurs in many ways. A business generally receives money in exchange for a product or service; however, the principles of exchange also apply to friendship, sports, or religious activities. People also conduct exchanges with their family members, friends, and nation.

You can exchange in abundance with your spouse, children, parents, employees, consumers, and other businesses. You can even provide a worthwhile exchange to humanity in general. There are no limits to the valuable things that can be exchanged.

Exchange in abundance is the key to expansion.

How to Eliminate Negativity

Set reasonable goals. Start with reasonable, achievable goals on the path toward larger goals. The satisfaction in reaching smaller goals first will motivate you to reach the next larger ones. Furthermore, as Stephen Covey states, "Begin with the end in mind."[63]

Turn "problems" into "challenges. Words are very powerful. Create a list of negative words or phrases that you use often and replace them with more positive ones. For example, instead of complaining about problems, refer to them instead as challenges. Eliminate the phrase *I should* from your self-talk, too, and replace it with *I could choose to....* The word *should* carries obligations, burdens, and resentments. On the other hand, the word *choose* puts you in control.

Reset your default answer. People who are naturally negative tend to use *no* as their first response to new ideas and experiences. Instead of *no*, default instead to *I'm not sure.* Then find a good reason to say *yes* to something.

Stand tall and smile. Historically, human beings have expressed power through large, open postures. Powerlessness is conveyed through body language, too—as in a shy person with slouched shoulders and downcast eyes. Standing tall with a smile, without looking down, makes you look bigger, more powerful, and more confident. It also sends the same message to your unconscious mind. For example, try feeling sad and depressed while you are smiling.

Be a critical thinker, not a critical person. If you are always seeing the negative in everything, the why things *cannot* be done, practice redirecting those thoughts by asking yourself, "What is true about this situation, dilemma, or person?" Remind yourself to always be a possibilities thinker, looking for opportunities for improvement.

Ask yourself, "What am I excited about doing today? Who can I encourage or serve today? What am I grateful for? Take the focus off yourself. Practice exchange in abundance as explained above.

Detox from bad news. I am not suggesting that you pretend that tragedy does not exist. But until you can build up some immunity to the negativity that the news can deliver, take a break from it. Resist the urge to read, view,or listen to the horrific details of the latest catastrophe. Instead, follow the tips and strategies available at sites such as Success.com/.

Eliminate your distortions. There are negative things in the world. Some

---

[63] *The Seven Habits of Highly Successful People* (New York: Simon and Schuster,1989).

"sky-is-falling" people are skeptical of focusing on the positive, for fear of being "delusional" and not seeing those very real negatives. So says Elizabeth Lombardo, who notes that we all have cognitive thinking distortions that can alter our perceptions of reality, perhaps causing the negatives to appear funhouse-mirror large.[64] A few common distortions include:

Mindreading: Assuming that you know what others think.

Fortunetelling: Predicting the future negatively and then reacting as if that prediction is imminent.

Dichotomous thinking: Assuming that everything is all or nothing.

Efficiency and Time Management

The main reason that people feel overworked, overloaded, or overwhelmed is not that they have too much work to do, but rather that they are working inefficiently. You can increase your accomplishments, be more productive, and have more free time if you replace two bad habits with one good one.[65]

Here are two bad habits to eliminate:

1. You are looking at a piece of work you are supposed to do—an e-mail, report, letter, program, interoffice communication, task assignment, request, whatever—and you put it aside. Later, you read it, digest it, think about doing it, consider the problems involved, and put it down. Nothing is accomplished. The whole procedure is a total waste of time. This is also referred to as an Open Cycle of Action, as discussed in Chapter 6, above.

2. You take a piece of work, decide you do not want to do it, and refer it to someone else, although it is your

---

[64]*A Happy You: Your Ultimate Prescription for Happiness* (Garden City, NY: Morgan James, 2010).
[65]This idea was first introduced to me by Meir Ezra.

responsibility. The other person eventually sends it back to you. This is a total waste of your time and theirs.

Here is one good habit to form:

Do it now! One of the best ways to cut your work in half is not to do it twice. Do every piece of work that comes your way *when* it comes your way, and not at some later point. Always take the initiative with action. This is known as a Closed Cycle of Action, as discussed in Chapter 6, above.

CYCLES OF ACTIONS Produce Time
CLOSED VS. OPEN
START: CHANGE: STOP = CLOSED
START: BEGIN CHANGE: UNFINISHED = OPEN
or
IDENTIFY: DO NOT START: PUT OFF = OPEN

The secret of efficiency is quite simple:

Step 1. Take all the e-mails in your inbox or a stack of papers or any kind of cluttered mess.

Step 2. Read the first item.

Step 3. Deal with it.

a. If the item is just for information or has no current real use, file it, store it, or discard it.

b. If you need to take action, do so right now. Persist until the job is completely *done*.

c. If you dislike the work involved, it is even more important that you do it *right now*.

d. Rewards of the do-it-now habit are numerous. For example, if you do your work in half the time, you will have extra time for new activities that you could use to increase your productivity.

Time and Priority Management

Time management is a misnomer. There is only priority management. We have no control over time, but we have lots of control over priorities. Commit yourself to investing your time in the most important priorities. Then bring that commitment alive by following the rest of the recommendations below.[66]

Make the Tough Decisions

Establish as your top priorities those items that are important, but not urgent. Decide which tasks and activities on your "to-do" list are truly goal-satisfying (the important ones), and which ones are only satisfying because you have to scratch them off your list (the urgent ones).

Rank your tasks in order of importance, not urgency.

Literally write the tasks on your planner from the most to the least important. Where two tasks have roughly the same importance, you may use urgency to determine which one has a higher priority.

Attend to your tasks in rank order.

Be proactive, not reactive. Make "appointments with yourself" to do what's most important, and write those appointments down in ink on your calendar. Close your door, if possible. If you can, flip your phone over to voicemail. Then perform the tasks on your list, starting with the most important one at the top.

First Things First

Stephen Covey, author of *The Seven Habits of Highly Effective People and First Things First*,[67] popularized the concept of a Time Management Matrix for prioritizing tasks, which was apparently first used by Dwight D. Eisenhower. The system advocates using four quadrants to determine the tasks you need to do and to decide in which order you should do them.

---

[66]Steve Marx, my friend, businessman, sales trainer, and author (now deceased) outlined these ideas to me in a memo after we had a discussion about this topic in relation to an upcoming meeting of the Tampa Bay Business Breakfast Group, also known as the BBG, of which we were both members.

[67](New York: Simon and Schuster, 1989).

Stephen Covey's 4 Quadrants

	Urgent	Not Urgent
Important	**Quad I** <u>Activities</u> • Crisis • Pressing Problems • Deadline Driven <u>Results</u> • Stress • Burn-out • Crisis management • Always putting out fires	**Quad II** <u>Activities</u> • Prevention, capability improvement • Relationship building • Recognizing new opportunities • Planning, recreation <u>Results</u> • Vision, perspective • Balance • Discipline • Control • Few crisis
Not Important	**Quad III** <u>Activities</u> • Interruptions, some callers • Some email, some reports • Some meetings • Proximate, pressing matters • Popular activities <u>Results</u> • Short term focus • Crisis management • Reputation – chameleon character • See goals/ plans as worthless • Feel victimized, out of control • Shallow or broken relationships	**Quad IV** <u>Activities</u> • Trivia, busy work • Some email • Personal social media • Some phone calls • Time wasters • Pleasant activities <u>Results</u> • Total irresponsibility • Fired from jobs • Dependent on others or institutions for basics

Figure 16: Stephen Covey's Four Quadrants

Quadrant 1 shows examples of items that are both important and urgent—that is, significant items that need to be dealt with immediately.

Quadrant 2 shows examples of items that are important but not urgent—that is, they are significant, but do not require immediate attention, although they need to be planned for. Covey stated that this is the quadrant we should focus on for long-term achievement of goals

Quadrant 3 shows examples of items that are urgent, but unimportant — that is, they should be minimized or eliminated because they are time stealers. They are the type of tasks for which Bob Carter said that "a lack of planning on your part does not necessitate an emergency on mine."[68]

Quadrant 4 shows examples of items that are neither important nor urgent—that is, they add little or no value to your tasks and are also not urgent. These are trivial time wasters.

---

[68]Bob Carter is a paleontologist, geologist, and marine biologist.

Habits are the compound interest of self-improvement. A small habit—when repeated consistently—grows into something significant.

People who excel tend to obsess over the details. People who struggle also tend to obsess over the details. The difference is what details they focus on. Minutiae vs polish. Most things don't matter—but when it does, you want to get the details right.

—James Clear[69]

In closing this section, here is a mantra that I created for myself to accomplish my goals and not be mired down in negativity. I say it to myself constantly:

Worry, fear, doubt, and all other negative thoughts are my enemies. They are destructive. When they present themselves, I dismiss them, excise them, and immediately replace them with positive thoughts, shifting my focus to actions that are constructive and will yield results.

---

[69]See https://jamesclear.com/.

CHAPTER 16

FITNESS, HEALTH, NUTRITION and WELL-BEING

The body is one part of a trilogy, including mind and emotions, that are all essential to enable a warrior to perform effectively in battle.

—Dan Millman[70]

It is our physical body that serves as the housing for our mind and spirit. It gives us the ability to perform and function in our day-to-day lives. The condition that we each choose to keep our bodies in, short of limitations that involve genetics or illness, either enables us or restricts us in how we live and impacts the tenure of our lives.

Fitness and exercise are crucial to one's physical and mental health. We need to *move!*

Long-term health can be elusive, yet maintaining it or mitigating the implications of being sickly or in a state of continual illness can be somewhat controlled. Our health is largely based on what and how we choose to eat and the degree to which we choose to exercise. Our health and well-being can be either positively or negatively affected by the manner in which we treat and respect our bodies through observing moderation in things that are otherwise harmful in excess, such as food, (overeating), alcohol, tobacco, and other drugs.

I have been on both ends of the spectrum with respect to fitness, nutrition,

---

[70]Adapted from Millman's *Way of the Peaceful Warrior* (Novato, CA: New World Library, 1980, 1984, 2000).

and health, so I have learned that being in a state of good health and fitness has a positive impact on all areas of my life, whereas being in a poor state-of health only leads to problems, both immediate and long-term. Some of those problems are probably ones that you would expect. However, others have had more far-reaching negative impacts on many areas of my life—effects that have required a great deal of "Iron Will" and hard work to overcome. It is my retrospective opinion that all of those effects could have been avoided by my maintaining a high level of fitness and nutrition, which in turn would have yielded better health and well-being.

Interestingly, some of our oldest religions have laws and traditions about nutrition. Many of those religions contain rules about fasting, vegetarianism, and diet. The authors of those ancient religious practices were aware of the benefits of good nutrition and the detriments of bad nutrition. Today, modern medical science is finally recognizing the power of conscientious nutrition as it affects health and longevity.

Exercise and the physical fitness that results from it not only enhance positive mental states but also offer longevity and mitigate the effects of many diseases and ailments. So, how do we permanently integrate fitness and good nutrition into our healthy lifestyles?

Well, most people are already aware of the general benefits of committing to such a program. However, some of us have a problem in implementing the program. Reaping the benefits of giving the program the highest priority requires a lifelong dedication. Thus, the thrust of this chapter is to provide a way for you to incorporate fitness and good nutrition into your life.

I would like to suggest a simple but effective means for you to do so. It is a concept that I use, and have been teaching to my daughter and son ever since they were old enough to understand my words. I call the theory "tricking your mind." Some of you may think, "Sure, easy to say, but hard to do." However, it is not at all hard to do. All it takes is persistence and repetition. It is perhaps the most effective means of accomplishing something that you will ever learn.

Even if you fall off your program, getting back on it is as easy as riding a bicycle. I have programmed my mind to absolutely *love* exercise and eating clean. When I am in the gym, I "reward" myself after my aerobic workout and my strength training workout with an extra period on the rowing machine. I am not suggesting that you push yourself beyond your limits. Rather, I am suggesting that, over and over again, you send your mind the message that daily exercise is one of the high points of your day. In other words, you reward your body with exercise.

You also reward your body with good eating habits and nutrition. With enough practice and repetition, this reward system will become an automatic part of your daily routine without thinking about it at all. It will not be something that you want to get out of the way, but rather something you *must* do because you *love* doing it. The focus needs to be on enjoying the activities of exercise and eating nutritious food. That will have positive benefits on all areas of your life, and will also serve as role modeling for others.

Create a sense of urgency. Develop your personal program and start implementing it *now*. Not tomorrow. Not next week. Not after that big upcoming party or vacation. And not after January 1 of whatever year is coming up. Start *immediately* by telling your mind over and over how much you are going to enjoy the process. Then start it.

I am reminded of an old saying about making money: "If you watch your pennies, the dollars will take care of themselves." The same applies to fitness, health, and nutrition. If you trick your mind by learning to love good nutrition and exercise, the results will just happen. As has been said many times, success is a journey, not a destination. Do it now. Make it happen. Make it fun.

As my friend Meir Ezra said in one of his podcasts, "Move to improve. Report to yourself. Be cause over your physical body. Tell it what to do."[71]

To summarize, some of the important benefits of fitness, nutrition, and well-being are:

1. *Weight Management:* Regular exercises and healthy eating will help you to avoid weight gain. Being physically active is necessary to reach or to maintain your weight targets, boost your immunity system, and increase your energy level. Modern studies indicate that you should do at least 150 minutes of exercise every week to stay active and fit. Along with exercising, of course, you should eat a balanced and calorie-managed diet. The right balance of carbs, greens, fruits, fats, and proteins boosts your energy level and keeps it going through your day.

2. *Mood Improvement:* A healthy lifestyle leads to a more relaxed mind and generally provides more energy for you throughout the day. Exercise and healthy eating also help you to improve your mood, boost your self-confidence, and overcome your stress.

3. *Disease Prevention:* Following a healthy lifestyle will help you to prevent or at least to manage certain diseases, such as heart disease, diabetes, high blood pressure, depression, body pains, etc. Although following a

---

[71]See MeirEzra.com/.

regimen of regular exercise and a balanced diet is not a cure-all, it will probably give you an edge in preventing or combating disease.

4. *Increased Energy:* Unhealthy eating most often carries with it a feeling of lethargy. On the other hand, a balanced healthy diet will give fuel to your body to perform all its functions. A healthy diet includes whole grains, lean meats or fish, low-fat dairy products (or no dairy products), fruits, and vegetables.

5. *Longevity:* Among the probable other benefits of adopting a healthy lifestyle are a longer life and overall well-being.

Guidelines from the American Heart Association (heart.org)

Recommendations for Adults

Get at least 150 minutes per week of moderate-intensity aerobic activity, or 75 minutes per week of vigorous aerobic activity, or a combination of both, preferably spread throughout the week.

Add moderate- to high-intensity muscle-strengthening activity (such as resistance or weights) on at least two days per week.

Spend less time sitting. Even light-intensity activity can offset some of the risks of being sedentary.

Gain even more benefits by being active at least 300 minutes (5 hours) per week.

Increase the amount and intensity of your exercise over time.

Recommendations for Kids

Children 3 to 5 years old should be physically active and have plenty of opportunities to move throughout the day.

Kids 6 to 17 years old should get at least 60 minutes per day of moderate- to vigorous-intensity physical activity, mostly aerobic.

Include vigorous-intensity activity on at least 3 days per week.

Include muscle- and bone-strengthening (weight-bearing) activities on at least 3 days per week.

Increase the amount and intensity of their exercise gradually over time.

CHAPTER 17

"IRON WILL"
A WORK IN PROCESS

Strength does not come from physical capacity. It comes from indomitable will.

—Mahatma Gandhi[72]

Life shrinks or expands in proportion to one's courage.

—Anaïs Nin[73]

I have been fascinated by a phenomenon I have observed in some others, but has frequently eluded me throughout my life. I have come to call this phenomenon "Iron Will."
Iron Will is the mastering of the ability to laser focus your thoughts in order to achieve your objectives. It is a strengthening of your mindset. Iron Will involves controlling your emotional responses to situations and also controlling the actions that result from those responses. Like an orchestration of a symphony, having an Iron Will enables you to remain in concert with your desired results. An Iron Will permits you to perform tasks successfully without being distracted. It is a mechanism that some people develop and others have innately. Having an Iron Will empowers you to be proactive rather than reactive to people, places, or things that you encounter throughout

---

[72]Available at: https://en.wikipedia.org/wiki/Mahatma_Gandhi/.
[73]*The Diary of Anaïs Nin* (New York: Harcourt Brace Jovanovich, 1996), vol. 3: 1939–1944).

your life. It is an ability to be in control most of the time without overreacting.

My friend Karen Meunier commented after reading this chapter, "I consider that 'Iron Will' is simply consistent free will."[74] That is an intriguing observation, since it recognizes that Iron Will means that we all *choose* how we respond to anything. If you have developed a strong set of guiding principles for your actions, then those principles will guide your free-will decisions, and thus your actions will be consistent and have integrity. A systematic approach to free-will decisions removes chaos and inconsistency. All systems are built from a series of interlinking and interrelated components. Perhaps, that is how the process of Iron Will evolves.

Your emotions serve as a catalyst for all of your actions, which can either charge you or discharge you. Will is a product of thought. Emotions stem from or are automatic responses to thoughts. Our emotional responses can cause us to react or overreact, when whatever the trigger may be is pulled to distract us from our direction or path. All too often, triggers yield passionate responses that may wreak havoc on what it is we want to accomplish or gain.

Karen Meunier suggests that our emotions are just symbols. If feeling sad or angry can be seen as a symbol, like a sign on the road that says there is a curve ahead, then the function of emotion may be to cause us to take note and take heed—to look out for something to which to respond. If one learns to take note of one's emotions, and moves past them to take action on their causative factors, then the emotions are only indicators of the causative factors, and in and of themselves powerless. We should recognize our emotions, honor them, and then look beyond them for their source, which is asking for our attention. Perhaps that is the art of having "Iron Will."

Iron Will can be trained, learned, and developed, as was exemplified by Michael Jordan, Arnold Schwarzenegger, Mohammed Ali, Benjamin Franklin, Albert Einstein, Thomas Edison, and Elon Musk, to name only a few examples. All of them proved that persistence is more powerful than perfection. None were perfect, but all were persistent and highly disciplined. Michael Jordan has been credited with saying, "Some people *want it* to happen. Some people *wish it* would happen. Others *make it* happen."[75] Iron Will can also be inherent, as depicted in the film *Africa: The Serengeti*, which portrays the survivors of a massive herd of wildebeests transcending the

---

[74]Karen Meunier and I first became acquainted when she became my assistant in 1976. Over the years, we became close friends and business associates.

[75]See http://en.wikipedia.org/wiki/Michael_Jordan/.

dangers, travails, and conditions on their annual migration.

Any people who have Iron Will realize that they are a force, a power to be reckoned with. The will that they have defines them and everything they encounter during their life journey. Constant and never-ending self-talk, as well as positive self-reinforcement, seem to be common characteristics-of people who have Iron Will.

As my friend Neil Cantor and I often said, whenever we were about to say goodbye to each other, "May the force be *you*."

When adversity of any kind presents itself—and it is inevitable that it will at various points in your life—you must recognize it for what it is. You must confront it, deal with it, and then steer through it, like professional athletes when they play though their pain. By not allowing yourself to be consumed by challenges, you will ultimately prevail. The saying "It is not what happens to me that matters, but how I deal with what happens to me" is very powerful and on point.

Behind the emotional responses you have to various situations, there is usually some type of fear. Perhaps it is an underlying fear that you may not even be consciously aware of. Nevertheless, it lies there beneath the surface, preventing you from transcending it and working through it. You must learn to own the fear instead of letting the fear own you. The latter is so often the case when Iron Will is absent. Eleanor Roosevelt stated the case perfectly when she said, "One gains strength, courage, and confidence by every experience in which you must stop and look fear in the face."[76]

To have Iron Will is to learn how to navigate the various events that life presents, in whatever form they may take, without interference from negative emotional responses that can distract you from accomplishing your objectives. It is your negative emotional responses that cause you to falter. It is the ability to process those negative emotions and move past them that allows you to succeed and prevail. As Dorothea Brande wrote, "All that is necessary to break the spell of frustration and inertia is to act as if it is impossible to fail. Failure is not an option."[77]

In *The Power of Myth*, a series of interviews with Joseph Campbell, Bill Moyers asks, "Do most of the stories of mythology from whatever culture say that suffering is an intrinsic part of life and that there is no way around it?" Campbell responds:

---

[76]Https://www.fdrlibrary.org/eleanor-roosevelt/.
[77]Dorothea Brande, *Wake Up and Live* (New York: Penguin, 1936).

They do. There is nothing I am aware of that will tell you, if you are going to live, you won't suffer. The mythologies throughout time and various cultures will tell you how to understand and bear and interpret suffering. That it will do. And when the Buddha says there is escape from suffering, the escape from sorrow is Nirvana. The Nirvana is a psychological position where you are untouched by desire and fear. When that happens, your life becomes harmonious, well-centered, and affirmative of life even with suffering.[78]

In my view, having or developing Iron Will is the difference between being excellent and being average. Individuals who learn how to have Iron Will achieve their aspirations and soar farther than those who permit their emotional responses to rule them.

What follows is something I call "The Process," which I have been developing in my ongoing attempt to develop Iron Will in my own life:

THE PROCESS
(or how to deal with and respond to a stressful situation)

- Feel it. (What does it feel like under the emotion?)
- Honor the feeling.
- Find the fear or stressful feeling and face it.
- Do the first small task to start to relieve it. (Eat the elephant technique: How do you eat an elephant? One bite at a time.)
- Recognize the tendency to overreact, and defer it.
- Do not allow emotions to cause obsession.
- Seek to fully understand the issue.
- Know that there is a course of action and correction for everything.
- Use the Serenity Prayer as an affirmation. ("Grant me the serenity to accept the things I cannot change, the courage to accept the things I can, and the wisdom to know the

---

[78]Program 5 of the PBS series *The Power of Myth*, Joseph Campbell and with Bill Moyers.

difference.")
- Ask, "What difference will this make years from now?"
- Don't just react, be patient until the time is right, and then be proactive.
- Realize that no matter how bad the incident or situation may seem, "this too shall pass."
- Repeat all of the above as many times as necessary.

The Process needs to be used throughout your life, especially during those times when circumstances call on you to have Iron Will. I, for one, have found that Iron Will can be quite difficult to develop and master. As a result, I have frequently found myself reacting in a weak and emotional manner, rather than with control and discipline, although I know the latter would produce much greater benefits. Nevertheless, even my conscious awareness of that does not seem to be enough to have Iron Will to use, so to speak, as an arrow in my quiver. However, I do intend to master it, no matter how elusive it has been.

What may appear to be random chaos in the universe is actually an orderly unfolding of cause and effect. The entire universe is an ordered exact infrastructure in a delicate balance. In my view, nothing happens by chance or by luck. Illness, injury, love, loss of love, lost moments of true greatness, death of a loved one, mistakes caused by whatever reasons, and or any other consequential experience all test and expand the limits, constraints, and boundaries of our souls. As a result, through our interactions with others and the circumstances we encounter, we forge our souls—not unlike the way steel is forged from the intense heat of a blast furnace when applied to iron ore. Without these tests throughout our lives, whatever they may be, life would be like a smoothly paved, straight, flat road to nowhere. It would be safe and comfortable, but dull and pointless. Helen Keller said, "Character cannot be developed in ease and quiet. Only through experience of trial and suffering can the soul be strengthened, ambition inspired, and success achieved."[79]

Since I am a student of aphorisms, I am aware of many that apply to the contexts we have been discussing. For instance:

- "What does not kill me will make me stronger." —Friedrich Nietzsche

---

[79]Available at: https://en.wikipedia.org/wiki/Helen_Keller/.

- If you have a problem that can be solved by money or effort, you don't have a problem.
- If you always do what you've always done, you will always get what you've always got.
- "Every minute of every day, I am getting stronger and stronger in every way." —Sarah Mahr (my mother)
- The will to win is not nearly as important as the will to prepare to win.
- Success can be best achieved when adequate preparation meets opportunity.

Merely knowing these words and concepts is not enough. In his book *Emotional Intelligence*, Daniel Goleman speaks about the dichotomy between logic and emotions.[80] We need to understand that, except for a very few of us who have Iron Will, we must all learn to recognize, understand, attempt to control, and work through the all-too-powerful effects that our emotions and emotional baggage have on virtually every aspect of our lives. But knowing is not ever enough. Acting with an Iron Will must underscore all of an individual's actions.

The great jurist Oliver Wendell Holmes once said, "I find the great thing in this world is not so much where we stand, as in what direction we are moving—we must sail sometimes with the wind and sometimes against it— but we must sail, and not drift, nor lie at anchor." Someone suggested to me after reviewing this chapter, "Inaction is a form of action, too, and its outcome is sometimes appropriate." Being willing to observe but not respond is a powerful tool used in Zen. A quote from an unknown source states, "Although we cannot adjust the wind, we can adjust our sails."

Many years ago, when I gave a copy of this chapter to a friend, who at the time was facing many challenges, she responded: "It is so interesting that I never really noticed how I handled disappointment. When I try to analyze my approach, I can only think that it's this long-ranging goal—that quest for justice—that keeps me going. And there is always music in my head that keeps me going as well." In essence, she was saying that she uses a conscious redirection of energy. In other words, she has learned how to use Iron Will for her own benefit and the benefit of those whose lives she touches.

---

[80]*Emotional Intelligence* (New York: Bantam, 1995).

This brings to mind concepts that I first learned from Napoleon Hill's book *Grow Rich with Peace of Mind*,[81] in which Hill identifies nine major motives that influence everything we do in various combinations. Seven of these motives are positive, and two are negative. The positive motives are:

1. the emotion of love.
2. the emotion of sex.
3. the desire for material gain.
4. the desire for self-preservation.
5. the desire for freedom of body and mind.
6. the desire for self-expression.
7. the desire for perpetuation of life after death.

The negative motives are:

8. the emotion of anger and revenge.
9. the emotion of fear.

Hill comments that "peace of mind is attained only by the exercise of the seven positive motives as a general pattern of life.... Sex is the greatest creative force of the universe. On its highest plane, it merges with love; but love can exist without being sexual. The mighty power of sex can be transmuted into action for the achievement of profound purpose." In essence, what Hill is writing about is the conscious redirection of energy, which is clearly an example of Iron Will.

When Peter Lowe was interviewing the actor Christopher Reeves after Reeves became a paraplegic from a horseback riding accident, Lowe started to ask, "Have you ever thought about how things might have been if—?" Before he could finish the question, Reeves took a breath, and said bluntly and emphatically, "Waste of time!" That is Iron Will.

Thoughts are things. They are tangible, real, and measurable. It is comforting to believe that thoughts are secret—that we can hide them from others. But actually our thoughts are always revealed by the actions to which

---

[81](New York: Penguin, 1967).

they must inevitably lead us.

Thought alone is insufficient to achieve results. We also need commitment, persistence, and belief to create results from thoughts. But thought is the driving force behind everything. By focusing our thoughts on a goal and committing ourselves to its fulfillment, we become like magnets, attracting people and events to bring our thoughts into being.

"Talking the talk" is not the same as "walking the walk." Iron Will is the ability to transcend whatever prevents you from talking *and* walking, regardless of the barriers that may be in your way.

Champions aren't made in gyms. Champions are made from something they have deep inside them: A desire, a dream, a vision. They have to have last-minute stamina, they have to be a little faster, they have to have the skill and the will. But the will must be stronger than the skill.

—Muhammad Ali

I cannot nor will not be ordinary. I have to keep training and seeking and growing. I have to stay hungry. It is my will, and so has become my nature.

—Arnold Schwarzenegger

The difference between a successful person and others is not a lack of strength, not a lack of knowledge, but rather a lack of will.

—Vince Lombardi

CHAPTER 18

GIVING

Oh, the gift, the gift they 'gee us. If only we could see us as others see us.

—An old Celtic saying

We visualize in metaphors, yet live and exist in reality. We are all a part of a vast interconnected universe of energy in a constant state of flow—a universe that by its very nature dictates the phenomena of cause and effect, action and reaction, or give and take.

The universe is a place of infinite abundance, from which each of us can claim our rightful share. Yet, we must also be cognizant of replenishing the universe. We must each be aware of cycles—the natural ebb and flow of the infinite ecosystem. As we cut down our forests to turn the trees into wood, paper, and other products, we must replant the seedlings to replace what we have claimed.

We are by our essence parts of a greater whole. We are members and participants of a magnificent infinite universe.

Plants take carbon dioxide from the air to exist, yet through photosynthesis they give back oxygen to the planet for all of us to breathe. Deceased organic matter decomposes and gives back to the Earth vital minerals. Herbs are refined to give animals and humans medicines, even new life in some instances. Everything is part of a circuitous and constant movement.

In *The Prophet*, Kahlil Gibran stated most eloquently that "there are those that give little of the much which they have, and they give it for recognition, and their hidden desire makes their gifts unwholesome. And there are those who have little and give it all. These are the believers in life and the bounty-of life, and their coffer is never empty."[82]

Years ago, a dear and special friend gave me a children's book called *The Giving Tree* by Shel Silverstein, which contained much adult wisdom.[83] My friend inscribed the book to me as follows: "To you, a very special friend, and to your children after you, may you never be afraid to love, live, and give." How appropriate and well chosen were her words to me, for you see, in my opinion, *love*, *live*, and *give* all have the same meaning. *The Giving Tree* is a wonderful story about the coexistence of a tree and a boy who grows to be an old man, and how the tree maintains happiness by giving to the boy and sharing with him throughout his life, providing for his needs as they change with his age.

Imagine, if you will, as John Lennon prodded us to do in his song *Imagine*, if all of us gave to each other and our universe unconditionally a part of everything we possess. The effects would create a balance and an environment for growth and development far beyond what we have yet recorded as a species—or for that matter, ever experienced.

Perhaps this concept is too ideal to ever be achieved; yet, the impact of the microcosm affecting the macrocosm is a known concept with great implications and benefits—meaning that each of us can participate in the giving. By simple acts of giving, each of us can have an effect for generations on the outcome of living—in some instances, by merely replenishing what we have taken.

I am reminded of a story about my parents, both of whom died at an early age. Years ago, when my brother was getting married, I asked my mother's brother, with whom I hadn't interacted in person since childhood because he had moved away, if he would take a few days off after the wedding and travel with me to where he and my mother had grown up, a small town in New York State near the Pennsylvania border. When he agreed, we drove together, with him recounting stories of their childhood. As we approached the neighborhood where they had lived, I noticed that it was very barren, a relatively poor area by the banks of the Allegheny River. Perhaps even in its day, it was at best a lower-middle-class to middle-class neighborhood.

On the final descent down to the river valley where their house was, I

[82]Kahlil Gibran, *The Prophet* (New York: Knopf, 1923).
[83]Shel Silverstein, *The Giving Tree* (New York: Harper & Row, 1964).

couldn't help noticing that there were no trees, except for one large sprawling green one at the bottom of the valley. When we pulled up in front of the house, which was quite dilapidated, there was the tree. I commented on it to my uncle, who informed me that my mother had planted it when she was a little girl. All these years later, it had survived and grown to be the only thing of beauty in an otherwise rundown neighborhood. My mother had given the area something precious, although she was unaware of its value at the time. I am sure that what she gave must have had an effect on many people. For me, my children, my extended family, and hopefully for their children, she set a standard that has caused each of us to emulate her by planting at least one tree wherever we have lived. (See Birthday Letter 2019 in the Appendix at the end of this book.)

It is so natural to give—perhaps more so than to receive. Many of the writings and teachings of the great religions contain parables to that effect. Yet, true giving is not to be construed as charity, although charity can certainly be a form of giving. For example, in Judaic teachings, there is no word for charity. Instead, the word *tzedakah* is used, which means "righteousness." Implicit, then, in Judaism is the concept that giving is not an exception, but the rule.

There is such a delicate balance in life as we know it. Certainly, giving ensures that the balance remains fine-tuned and infinite.

There is an old proverb that states, "A torch is not diminished, though it kindles a million lights. So, will he not lose who gives to others."

To reiterate a concept stated earlier, *the universe is a place of abundance.* It is ready to share with those of us who claim the opportunity to reward ourselves and those we choose to touch. Nevertheless, we must remain cognizant of what the reward will be that will be available for those yet to be born. How will they be greeted by the universe, and what opportunities will there be for them to become and to grow?

The commitment we maintain to giving can be likened to flowers planted on the landscape of life. The seeds have been sown in us and in our children, which are our parents' and grandparents' contribution to the future flowers that will need to be planted. The brushstrokes now must come from our hands, to keep the palate of the landscape alive, vital, and full of color. Yet, what of the future flowers that will need to be planted?

By our example, we must teach the next generation to give. We must replenish. We must always continue to plant the seeds of new flowers—for it will be our children, grandchildren, great-grandchildren, and beyond who will watch them bloom with pride, joy, and happiness, serving as an example to do the same for those yet to come.

With respect to our interpersonal relationships with friends, family members, lovers, and so on, as will be discussed in greater detail below, I have learned that at the very essence and core of truly successful relationships, there is a commitment to unconditional giving. Think of the possibilities that embracing that concept would have if it were applied to our relationships with our significant others, our children, our family members, and our special friends. We can accept them for who and what they are, and love them for it. We can give of ourselves rather than materially. That offers us the framework for happiness and success.

Consider this example of random giving. Years ago, I was on an airplane flying from Tampa to Phoenix. It was an early morning flight that was not heavily booked. Sitting across the aisle from me in the window seat, with both seats next to her vacant, was a woman in her late forties or early fifties, who had a pained look on her face. I was spread out in my row of seats, working, but from time to time I couldn't help noticing her, for she was obviously distraught about something.

Every once in a while, she brushed tears away from her eyes. At one point, she actually sobbed aloud, then attempted to regain her composure when she thought someone might notice. About midway through the flight, I wrote the following note to her:

> *Hi. Please don't be offended by this. I know it is not my place and do apologize for noticing, but I am sorry you are sad and sincerely hope your pain goes away soon. Stay strong! No matter what it is, trust that it will get better. Sincerely, just a person who knows what pain can feel like, and wishes you well.*

As I got up from my seat on the way to the restroom, I silently handed her the note. When I returned, she looked at me with moist eyes and silently mouthed the words, "Thank you for caring."

I sat back in my seat and had no further interaction with her for the rest-of the flight. When the plane landed, our eyes met and I gave her a thumbs up sign with a big smile. She returned it with a slight smile and nodded her head in acknowledgment.

My dear friend and Comrade in Arms Richard Gorbaty recently asked me if I were familiar with the story of the starfish. I told him I wasn't, so he shared the following with me:

94

There were hundreds of starfish washed upon a beach. A little boy playing nearby comes upon them and picks one up and throws it back in the water. A man sees the little boy and says to him, "You're wasting your time. You can't help all those starfish." The little boy replies as he throws another back into the water, "Well, I just helped that one."

The act of giving can move the needle for many. However, that movement begins with just giving to one person, place, or thing, which is usually a simple action or random act of kindness. The result of that simple act or action can be a rippling effect that makes a difference to so many.

Giving can take many forms in life. Its rewards are shared equally by the giver and the receiver.

Figure 17: Giving Jan Canty

BE | DO | HAVE

CHAPTER 19

RELATIONSHIPS

No man is an island, entire of itself; every man is a piece of the continent, a part of the main.

—John Donne

The above quote speaks to the necessity of our interpersonal relationships. Yet, why are relationships the most challenging aspect of our lives?

As we get older and gain more experience, our relationships seem to get more difficult to identify, arrange, maintain, and understand—a condition I refer to as "I Am Us." In my opinion, the process should be just the opposite. As we mature, our advancing wisdom should make our relationships more important to us. Shouldn't they be *easier* to identify, arrange, maintain, and understand? Why is that the exception for most of us, and not the rule?

To answer these questions, we need to start by looking within ourselves. All relationships with others begin with our relationship with ourselves. The quality of our relationship with ourselves dictates the quality of our relationships with others. That is not to say that good relationships require reinventing ourselves to fit into them. Rather, they require us to bring a complete and whole individual to them. Imagine two half-circles coming together to form a whole. Each half of the circle is dependent on the other to be a complete circle. In this scenario, the halves need each other. One without the other is only a half. Now picture two whole circles, each one complete by itself. When these two circles come together and superimpose themselves on each other, the result is a stronger circle than either one alone. They are not dependent on each other, but are rather interdependent together.

Relationships, whether platonic or romantic, whether with members of the same or the opposite sex, whether with younger, older, or similarly aged individuals, are never found outside of yourself. They always begin within yourself, and then later are manifested to include others. *I Am Us.*

A part of the answer to the questions posed above is that too many of us rely on others to bring completeness to ourselves. That rarely works, and even in the rare instances when it does, it is usually ephemeral. Once we have embarked on a decision to be whole unto ourselves, perhaps the next single most important factor in identifying, arranging, maintaining, and understanding relationships is *attitude*. The right personal attitude can serve like a magnet attracting others to it. The wrong personal attitude can repel people from it. We must realize that the energy is within each of us to be successful in all areas of our lives, including our relationships. The fact is that it is *us* and the choices we make—not fate, anyone else, or even a Supreme Being—that dictates or controls our destinies, including our destinies with others.

Jim Rohn, an entrepreneur, author, and motivational speaker, stated, "One person caring about another represents life's greatest value."[84] But how do we make that work? This brings to mind the following poem that I wrote:

IF ONLY

If only.... If only.... If, If, If..............
If only it were possible to be everything we each need, want, and expect.
To be the exact perfect person who paints the colors on the pictures we each have outlined as desires in our hearts;
If only it were possible to transcend hurt, confusion, and fear, with strength direction, and acceptance of each other as we are, even with our limitations;
If it were, we could always be perfect together for each other and for ourselves;
If it were, those tender moments of intimate embrace and connection would last every moment;

---

[84]https://www.jimrohn.com/.

If it were, our celebration of love would never cease;

If it were, our passion could always be sustained, never to diminish or be challenged, only to grow and enhance passion in all that we are and are to become;

If it were, we would always just understand and acquiesce for each other on issues that are really not so important in the real scheme of things that are;

If it were, we would each only give to the other. Taking would be replaced by receiving without expectation;

If it were, we would always strive to act in harmony, only allowing outside conflict and discourse to be a venue for growth, discovery, and deeper mutual bonding;

If it were, we would facilitate each other's growth emotionally and spiritually. Security and strength would come from within, and there would be no emptiness inside to have each other fill, because self-completion would be provided by each, not for each, but enhanced by each;

If it were, love, respect, and trust would transcend every aspect of fear;

If it were, our interaction together would be enabling, allowing two individuals to achieve personal strength and continual growth, bringing those strengths to an even stronger union, where individual vulnerabilities are protected by a "safe harbor" of being strong together;

If it were.... If only.... If, If, If...............

Yet, perfection by definition does not exist in any form anywhere in the universe. It is contrary to all of the physical laws as we know them..., so it seems that the closest we can come is to try as best we can, to persist, to communicate, to strive, to dream, to compromise, to try again and again and again, and then once more again..., always to believe we can.

If it were, If only, If, If If.... Well, maybe..., so then why not...?

If we agree that the starting point of any quality relationship lies within ourselves, we must also realize that it takes more than the efforts of one person to make a relationship work. That is not to say that one person cannot initiate a relationship; however, at some point, there has to be reciprocal giving and a desire for the relationship to flourish and grow.

Relationships with family members, friends, lovers, and ourselves must be cultivated like a garden, sometimes requiring great patience. Time, effort, and imagination must be summoned constantly to keep those relationships flourishing. Once again, this is an example of the Go-Grow-Quo Theory that I wrote about earlier. Nothing remains constant. Start every relationship by first being loyal to yourself. Then, through loyalty to your family members, friends, and loved ones, you will reap the rewards and benefits of quality interpersonal relationships.

To be infinitely more gratifying and successful, relationships should be based on preferences rather than demands. To quote Ken Keyes, Jr., from his book, *Your Life Is a Gift*:

> Instead of trying to wear yourself out trying to change the people in your life, give yourself the option of changing your addictive demands…, your requirements or expectations that you place upon them…. As you let go of your addictive demands, you can still have preferences. You can prefer that something happen in a certain way, but if it doesn't happen, you can remain happy, because it is not a condition of your happiness. The preference is a desire that doesn't make you feel unhappy or upset if it isn't met.[85]

So, by starting within yourself, by changing your own programming, you can affect how relationships with others will evolve and be sustained. What happens is that by incorporating into your own programming the preferences that Ken Keyes, Jr., writes about, you are able to meet people in relationships with understanding, love, acceptance, and happiness, rather than through negative emotional responses.

In practice, relationships can be romantic or platonic, passionate or subdued, exciting or boring, fulfilling or lacking, friendly or hostile, understanding or imposing, meaningful or superficial, giving or selfish, stimulating or depressing. Relationships can cultivate personal growth or smother it. Relationships encompass a full spectrum of human behavior and communion. As a matter of fact, it is quite possible that interpersonal relationships are the key to this earthly existence.

---

[85]Available at https://en.wikipedia.org/wiki/Ken_Keyes_Jr./.

In the first book of his trilogy *Conversations with God*, Neale Donald Walsch states:

> All human actions are motivated at their deepest level by one of two emotions, fear or love.... There is no other human motivation, and all other ideas are but derivatives of these two. Think on it deeply, and you will see that it is true. This is the sponsoring thought. It is either a thought of love or fear.... It is the raw energy that drives the human experience.... Human behavior produces repeat experiences; it is why humans love to destroy, then love again: always there is the swing from one emotion to the other. Love sponsors, fear sponsors, love sponsors, fear sponsors..., so it is in the moment you pledge your highest love, you greet your greatest fear. For the first thing you worry about after saying, "I love you," is whether you will hear it back. And if you hear it back, then you immediately begin to worry that the love you have just found, you will lose. And so, all action becomes a reaction, defense against loss.... Yet, if you knew who you are, that you are the most magnificent, most remarkable, the most splendid being God has created, you would never fear.[86]

The challenge we each face, however, regardless of relationships or the lack thereof, is to rise above whatever circumstances we find ourselves in, and become fully responsible for all of our own actions with whatever resources we have. We, not fate, control our own destinies. We must consciously choose to focus on the positive and transcend the negative. It is then that we naturally create an energy that pulls others to us, without our seeking them. As Richard Bach writes in his book *Illusions*, "Every person, all the events in your life, are there because you have drawn them there. What you choose to do with them is up to you."[87]

My personal experiences pertaining to relationships among so many other areas of my life have been exponentially enhanced by the incredible relationship with my lady, life mate and partner Julia Kristmundsdottir, which as of the date of this writing has now been for over 13 years.

I Am Us.

---

[86]*Conversations with God* (New York: Penguin Putnam, 1996).
[87]*Illusions* (New York: Dell, 1977).

CHAPTER 20

INTIMACY

Float like a butterfly, sting like a bee.

—Mohammed Ali

Passion! The energy and experiences of the forces unleashed by the intimacy and sexual interaction between two lovers are the strongest physical, emotional, and spiritual feelings we can ever experience. We literally experience magical moments, fulfillment, and completeness through intimate interaction—although in its most basic forms, intimacy is the means by which we perpetuate life's longing for itself, through amazing physical stimuli and drives.

However, intimacy is not only something that people can experience on a physical level. Fortunately, it can take on multidimensional characteristics when it embraces emotional fulfillment as well. It is the ultimate level of communication and connection between two people.

Although there can be high levels of excitement through experiencing many different partners, there is nothing—absolutely nothing—as amazing, wondrous, and satisfying as a passionate, loving, highly sexually charged, monogamous romantic relationship. Once it is experienced, nothing less can or will suffice. Without intimacy, we drift aimlessly, searching for it—perhaps even unaware that we are drifting, but nevertheless frustrated and unfulfilled.

How we feel and act intimately impacts many, if not all, areas of our lives. So strong and compelling is the desire for intimate contact that many individuals freely risk their lives and reputations to find it. When intimacy is an obsession or addiction, it can have negative manifestations, such as the many scandals that occupy so much of the media coverage these days.

When passion and intimacy are absent from monogamous relationships, that can lead to affairs, which in turn can break up otherwise satisfying unions. Physical intimacy is one of the strongest feelings we have. However, it can either take us to higher levels or consume us in obsessions.

In *Think and Grow Rich*, Napoleon Hill writes about the power of sexual transmutation—that is, channeling the powers of sexual energy into other areas of personal goal achievement.[88] We are naturally stimulated by the urge for sex. The ecstasy and longing of romantic sex with our true mates was perhaps best explained by Plato in the *Symposium*:

> The sexes were not two but three; there was man, woman, and the union of the two.... Initially the union of the two was androgynous in nature until the fabled Zeus decreed that they be divided to diminish their power and potential threat to his fellow Gods.... After the division into two parts, each yearned and desired for the other half.... When they came together, entwined in mutual embrace, they longed to grow back into one.... When one half meets his/her other half, the pair are lost in amazement, love, friendship, and intimacy.... These are the people that spend their whole lives together..., for the intense yearning which each of them has towards the other does not appear to be the desire of mere lover's intercourse, but rather of something else which the soul of either desires.[89]

Two lovers experiencing and expressing their love for each other sexually is the epitome of romantic interaction and transcends simple metaphor. Nevertheless, there have always been five things that were special to me as a musician and creative romantic soul. I found using them to be appropriate in creating the prose poem that follows. Can you tell what the five things are?

---

[88]*Think and Grow Rich* (Meridian, CT: The Ralston Society, 1937).
[89]Available at https://en.wikipedia.org/wiki/Symposium_(Plato)/.

The Five

As a stone cast amidst the serenity of still waters produces ripples
some small, some soft and gentle, some large,
some intense and reaching far across its depths and dimensions....
As raindrops fall and gently caress the leaves of trees, the blades of grass
and glisten with rays of light illuminating....
As a butterfly floats on ribbons of air, like a gentle breeze blowing a ribbon on a young girl's hair....
As a sunset kisses the horizon, and its touch gently lingers on the cheek of the sky at dusk....
As a rainbow's colors are presented as brushstrokes from a vast palette of magic against an azure blue canvas....
As the light, the instant after a rainfall, freshens and serves to accentuate the beauty that lies beneath what is always there....
As the force and power of great waves cascade the sands of the shore,
carrying with them everything from within....
So, too, are those supreme moments of amazement and wonder spent together entwined in the essence of mutual
embrace, connection, and oneness.

Figure 18: Brett Jordan Unsplash

CHAPTER 21

SPIRITUALITY [TO BE CONNECTED]

The spiritual self completes the trinity of the three selves. It manifests qualities of selfless courage, love, compassion, wisdom, altruism, and joy. It serves as a "cheerleader to the soul."

—Dan Millman[90]

There are more things in heaven and earth, Horatio, than are dreamt of in your philosophy.

—William Shakespeare[91]

If I do good, I get good. If I do bad, I get bad, and that is my religion.

—Abraham Lincoln[92]

---

[90]Available at https://en.wikipedia.org/wiki/Dan_Millman/.
[91]Hamlet to Horatio in *Hamlet*, I.v.167–168.
[92]Abraham Lincoln was the 16th President of the United States.

If the doors of perception were cleansed, everything would appear to man as it is, infinite.

—William Blake[93]

What is strange, what is marvelous, is not that God really exists. The marvel is that such an idea, the idea of the necessity of God, could have entered the head of such a savage and vicious beast as man; so holy it is, so moving, so wise, and such a great honor it does to man.

—Fyodor Dostoevsky[94]

This is my simple religion. There is no need for temples, no need for complicated philosophy. Our own brain, our own heart is our temple. My religion is very simple. My religion is kindness.

—Dalai Lama[95]

Having and maintaining a spiritual awareness is congruent with being an integral and connected part of the multiverse. Organized religion, although often confused with spirituality, is partially, in my view, an earthly formula devised by human leaders to control the masses.[96] Next, mankind should achieve a state of harmonious coexistence and mutual respect with all living things, and thus a state of spiritual being. The problem is that, more often than not, most contemporary religious practices have fallen short of their purpose. Although they have many customs and traditions, many religions have left a void in the realm of spiritual fulfillment. Of course, individuals who understand and relate to the practices of various religions can,

---

[93] Available at https://en.wikipedia.org/wiki/The_Marriage_of_Heaven_and_Hell/.

[94] Available at https://en.wikipedia.org/wiki/The_Brothers_Karamazov/.

[95] Available at https://en.wikipedia.org/wiki/Dalai_Lama/.

[96] I have always maintained that the key of existence on the physical plane is interpersonal relations between and among living things.

and in many instances do, find spiritual connectivity. Many, however, do not. For example, while I was growing up and learning Hebrew prayers, I would ask my mother the meanings of words I didn't understand. She would tell me that it didn't matter if I knew the meanings-of the words. All that mattered was that I said them. That is the way she was taught, and that's what she thought was important. The implications are obvious.

In *The Inner Reaches of Outer Space*, Joseph Campbell wrote:

> Reviewing with unprejudiced eye the religious traditions of mankind, one becomes very soon aware of certain mythic motifs that are common to all, though differently understood and developed in the differing traditions; ideas for example, of a life beyond death, or of malevolent and protective spirits.[97]

The Messianic Age is prayed for by many people in modern-day religions. I do not believe that Age will necessarily be marked by the coming of a messianic individual or entity, but rather by a state of universal awareness, which will prevail as we continue to evolve as a species, physiologically, intellectually, and spiritually. People journey on a quest for an understanding of spiritual realities that are within each of them, yet also beyond each-of them.

Religion as we know it in the many forms it has taken and continues to take has enabled mankind to exist and co-exist throughout the unexplained and irrational wonder of life. It seems to me that the various forms that religion takes serve as evolutionary tools as human beings advance to the next step of their evolution. For example, humans had to be evolved enough and had to have experienced enough history and lessons to be able to comprehend and receive the Ten Commandments, a code of conduct and life that is almost six thousand years old. Metaphorically, we had to go through the industrial revolution before we were able to go through and experience the technological revolution and onto the information revolution we are in now. There are many people who believe, and in my opinion rightly so, that as we advance and discover more in the technological and scientific realm, our spiritual awareness will likewise progressively take on new dimensions. As of yet, however, our still somewhat primitive state and position on the vast

---

[97]*The Inner Reaches of Outer Space* (New York: A. van der Marck, 1986).

evolutionary ladder of existence, albeit advanced compared to our human experience and history, limit our intellectual ability to comprehend. The possibilities are actually limitless of what reality could be or may be.

It is beyond humans' ability to comprehend life outside the confines of their experiences, although their comprehensions have been changing and evolving throughout the history of the planet. Human viewpoints are predicated on the experiential phenomena of mankind and the individual datapoints we allow ourselves to be influenced by. The Kabbalah, a collection of Judaic writings on mysticism, alludes to this throughout its teachings.[98]

As a species, we have engrained in our DNA the influences of the tribalism that we inherited from our ancestors. Each of us has by default a vested belief system that our varied tribal customs and practices have dictated over time.[99] One of our inherent problems, however, is that many practices and customs that we have inherited have not evolved at the same pace or in step with the evolution and changes that have taken place since they were originally conceived. The Kabbalah teaches that God is an ever-changing force, that the God of today is not the God of yesterday, nor the God of tomorrow. Nothing remains constant. In the words of Rabbi Allen S. Maller, "Birth and death, creation and destruction seem an inevitable part of existence. Nothing lasts forever in the form(s) they currently hold. Even stars eventually burn out and die."[100]

Everything is in a constant state of change, so too spirituality. However, throughout recorded time, religions have placed a special emphasis on certain aspects of religious practices, according to the perceived needs of their members. These practices have been administered to the masses by the leaders of various religions or smaller denominations within larger religions. An example would be when King David stressed certain principles of conduct and selectively focused on only some of the commandments, *mitzvoth*[101] in an attempt to improve interpersonal relationships. He addressed the needs of his

---

[98]Literally, the Hebrew word *Kabbalah* means "tradition" or "the tradition of things divine."

[99]In *The Inner Reaches of Outer Space: Metaphor as Myth and Religion,*(New York: A. van der Marck, 1986), Joseph Campbell, wrote, "The historically conditioned field of thought and language by which our lives are shaped are indeed historically conditioned, whereas the psychosomatic entity that is everywhere being shaped, namely the bioenergetic system of the one species, homo sapiens, is and has been for some forty millennia a constant."

[100]Rabbi Allen S. Maller, *God, Sex and Kabbalah* (Los Angeles, CA: Ridgefield Publishing Company, 1983).

[101]*Mitzvoth* is the Hebrew word for the commandments or good deeds enumerated in the Torah. There are 613 of them listed in The Five Books of Moses.

people at the time, as he believed them to be. Unfortunately, most of us are influenced by the dictates and pressures that are imposed on us by our tribal customs, families, etc. This does not take into account the fact that individual differences in talents, personality, and sensory and intellectual abilities create differences in opportunity, needs, desires, and viewpoints.

For example, the Jewish laws of *mitzvoth*, or the practice of the Christian Christmas spirit that prevails during that time of year, or the current metaphor contained on t-shirts and various other paraphernalia, "W.W.J.D." (What would Jesus do?) are all more spiritual than religious in nature. Therein are keys and signs of the gradual movement toward the spiritual state-of-awareness that we as a species have labeled the coming Messianic Age. Perhaps it was even necessary for human beings, based on their intellectual, emotional, and spiritual development, to have transcended idolatry. Nevertheless, they still required a physical representation of themselves to relate to in order to be able to embody the abstract concept of Godliness. Hence, Jesus, Buddha, Mohammed, and others came at times that the tribes they impacted had imagery to help define what was too abstract to otherwise have a meaningful influence.

In my view, human beings are slowly coming together as a unified population on the planet Earth, and tribalism will eventually dissipate. In the words of Maller:

> There is only one God, but there is more than one religion....
> There are many paths to God and many ways to worship the
> Infinite. People's manner of worshiping the Infinite depends on
> their culture, their family, and their own personality.[102]

Possibly, in a few thousand Earth years or so, this dissipation of tribalism will take us to another level of awareness—perhaps to a closer connection to the forces of life that are beyond our as yet undeveloped mental and sensory ability to truly comprehend what God is and what we are really just a small part of.

In my view, the possibility of extraterrestrial life forms elsewhere in the universe does not provide meaningful answers to the question of what God is

---

[102]Rabbi Allen S. Maller, *God, Sex and Kabbalah* (Los Angeles, CA: Ridgefield Publishing Company, 1983).

or may be. If other life forms do exist, they, too, must be subjects of a greater whole—a whole and divinity that is beyond our still evolving ability to comprehend. A spark of what many human beings believe is the divine is inside each of us as a part of our being. Its existence is perhaps an explanation of the state of spiritual euphoria that believers experience during those times when they connect with it.

The essence of the divine lies within all things, organic and inorganic, animate and inanimate, known and unknown. We are all part of an infinite whole. Our connection with the whole does not necessarily lie within a physical structure, but is much deeper in our spiritual link with all things. Our behavior, our thoughts, our beliefs, our actions, and our inactions are all microcosms that affect all of the other components of the universe, the macrocosm. They are like the tiniest ripples in a still body of water. They may be tiny, but they are a force nevertheless, which serves to displace the stillness that existed before it. So, too, is each of our individual spiritualities.

Deepak Chopra has written:

> The physical universe is nothing other than the Self curving back unto Itself, to experience itself as spirit, mind, and physical matter. The source of all creation is divinity (or the spirit); the process of creation is divinity in motion (or the mind); and the object of creation is the physical universe (which includes the physical body).[103]

In *The Astrological Secrets of the Hebrew Sages*, Rabbi Joel C. Dobbin wrote that "there is a divine balance that links God, man, and the universe into one balanced process which never ends in life or on other planes of awareness of life."[104]

Neale Donald Walsch wrote:

> You are a threefold being. You consist of body, mind, and spirit. You could also call these the physical, non-physical, and the meta-physical. This is the Holy trinity, and it has been

---

[103]https://www.deepakchopra.com/articles/did-life-create-the-universe/.
[104]Rabbi Joel C. Dobbin, *The Astrological Secrets of the Hebrew Sages* (New York: Inner Traditions, 1983*)*.

called by many names. Some of your theologians have called this father, son, and the Holy Spirit. Your psychiatrists have recognized this triumvirate and called it conscious, subconscious, and super-conscious. Your philosophers have called it the id, the ego, and the super-ego. Science calls this energy, matter, and antimatter. Poets speak of mind, heart, and soul. New Age thinkers refer to body, mind, and spirit. Your time is divided into past, present, and future. Space is divided into there, here, and the space in between. The three aspects of you are actually three energies: thought, word, and action. The entire structure of everything in the universe is thus linked. The process of creation starts with thought, an idea, a conception, a visualization. Thought is the first level of creation. Next comes the word: everything you say is an expressed thought. It is creative and sends forth creative energy into the universe. Words are more dynamic than thoughts, because words are a different level of vibration than thoughts. Words disrupt the universe with greater impact. Words are the second level of creation. Third comes action. Actions are words in motion. Words are expressed thoughts. Thoughts are formed ideas. Ideas are combined energies. Energies are released forces. Forces are existent elements. Elements are particles of God , portions of all, the stuff of everything"[105]

In essence, spirituality may be the sharing in fellowship between mankind and the divine. Spiritual connection enables human beings to achieve a euphoric and peaceful state. In Psalm 23, God is a shepherd who makes us lie down in still waters to restore our souls. The beginning of all relationships— whether between man and woman, man and man, woman and woman, city and state, state and nation, nation and other nation, planet and universe—is based on knowledge that leads to wisdom, which is shared through communication. Some people believe that the fear of God is the beginning-of wisdom.[106] Knowledge of God has been likened to a circle. Our knowledge-of

---

[105]Neale Donald Walsch, *Conversations with God*, book 1 (New York: Putnam, 1996).

[106]Primitive human beings, fearing the forces of nature, worshipped them. That was a part of the evolution of mankind's knowledge, discoveries, and wisdom, which is still in its relative infancy.

God and divinity is what is inside the circle. Outside the circle is what we don't know. The more we know as we evolve and develop, the bigger the circle becomes. However, the result is an awareness that there is so much that we don't know *outside* the circle. Incidentally, this also applies to technology, scientific knowledge, and medical discovery, as can readily be demonstrated by the leaps we are taking today in all of those areas. Human creativity in these areas has greatly improved the quality of human life by reducing our helplessness before the forces of nature.

Notwithstanding where we are, however, and what wondrous things we have discovered in those areas, we have merely scratched the surface. There is a progressive effect with discovery and technology, although it is always unpretentious in the beginning stages. Our human existence perhaps began with the use of a stick to pick up small insects for food. Then we moved on to using stones or clubs that extended our hitting range. Over time, and with many more advances in gradual technological evolution, that led to today's internet. Our boundaries on Earth have been shrunk dramatically, for we have linked the far reaches of our planet to new levels of communication and shared information. All of our known information has been catalogued and is now readily available to everyone. This latest technological advance is enabling the synergistic development of new technology in all fields. This serves to meld our individual talents and powers to reach out to the galaxies as a unified population of the planet Earth—our next step in the evolutionary journey of our species. This latest step, as advanced as it may seem to us now, is yet merely another beginning, and is likewise as modest as our other early stages.

In the words of Maller:

> Spiritual growth must be developed.... The coming of the Messianic Age, contrary to common belief, is not a present from God. Rather, it is a goal humanity can achieve in partnership with God when we struggle vigilantly and persistently without despairing over our obstacles or becoming complacent over our successes.[107]

---

[107]Rabbi Allen S. Maller, *God, Sex and Kabbalah* (Los Angeles: Ridgefield Publishing Company, 1983).

In *Toward a Meaningful Life: The Wisdom of the Rebbe*, Simon Jacobson writes:

> There is a built-in dichotomy between the tangible nature of the body and the transcendent nature of the soul. Look closely at the flame of the candle, and you will see the approximation of your soul, the flame licking the air, reaching upward…, while the wick pulls it back to Earth.[108]

The conflict between feeding the sensory desires of the body and nourishing the ethereal yearnings for connection of the soul is the challenge we are presented when we seek spiritual fulfillment. To be spiritual is not only to learn to transcend the desires of our sensual appetites. Rather, in addition it is to obtain and maintain a connection with the divine, having an awareness-of everything else we share in the universe with a reverence for the essence-of everything that is a part of each of us.

I once had a very interesting dream, in which a born-again Christian friend of mine appeared to me. He had died two years before, but in my dream, he appeared at the entranceway to a door in a building I owned, which I was trying to repair. He said he had to whisper a song in my ear, and then he asked me to sing it back to him, since he knew I was formerly a musician. Then he asked me to sign the back of an ancient medal he had with Jesus on it. When he leaned over to my ear and started to sing the song, I felt euphoria going through me as he hummed the words. But then my deceased father instantly appeared and pulled me away. He sat me down in a bedroom with him, at which point my deceased mother came in, but my father refused to talk while she was there. When she went into another room, my father said in his soothing deep voice, the following words:

> Fear not the trials and the stress. Do not seek a premature end to the life you have been given. Experience it, whatever it may be for all that it is. Have faith and surrender yourself to believe in the powers that have given it to you. Listen to the murmuring that lies within your heart. Live, love, believe, and

---

[108]Simon Jacobson, *Toward a Meaningful Life: The Wisdom of the Rebbe* (New York: William Morrow, 1995).

be reverent to all the forces that have created you. Tell these words to your children, your brother and sister, and teach them to others along your way.

He then disappeared, and the words repeated themselves to me three times from a very spiritual sounding voice that surrounded me, as if in an echo chamber. Then I woke up. Those were my father's exact words, which I immediately wrote down.

On a website entitled Cosmiclight.com, it is said:

The purpose of metaphysics is often misunderstood among religious thinkers. This is unfortunate. When a teaching becomes so dogmatic that it loses track of any sort of metaphysical understanding of the transcendental omnipresence, it becomes essentially stagnant and blind to what a spiritual universe is all about. Those familiar with the ancient mystical philosophies do not have a problem with the abstract universal principles of metaphysics and how they relate to the parochialism of theological traditions. Ideally, the ultimate goal of *any* theological tradition should be to bring the individual seeker to a state of spiritual awareness in which *all* such theological traditions are assimilated, and at the same time, not needed in their dogmatic form.[109]

Albert Einstein wrote in *The World As I See It*, "The most beautiful experience we can have is the mysterious. It is the fundamental emotion that stands at the cradle of true art and true science."[110]

Haridas Chaudhuri stated:

Individuality…is an active center of dynamic self-expression of the Supreme. In that case, true wisdom cannot consist in mere self-negation in an absolute void, or in self-annihilation in the formless absolute. The path of wisdom rather lies in the

---

[109]Available at http://www.cosmiclight.com/.
[110]Available at https://en.wikipedia.org/wiki/The_World_as_I_See_It_(book)/.

realization of one's essential oneness with the whole of existence and in the reconstruction of one's life on the basis of that realization.[111]

The Learning Channel aired an interesting television documentary about scientific advancements that will enable and ultimately lead to the colonization of the moon. Technology that builds on advances that proceeded it will be used to create, in a relatively short time-frame, a self-contained colony, more or less the way Las Vegas was.[112] We have the technology, engineering skills, and abilities now to construct megastructures. Those structures are self-contained, providing their own sources of air, water, power, plant life, and a myriad of uses for employees, customers, and visitors.

On the moon, there could be living environments, areas for farming and growth of plant life for photosynthesis, synthetic sunlight, work areas, entertainment areas, water processing, exercise facilities, and the list goes on and on to include all other areas required by humans to exist, live, work, and play. The possibilities are limitless. If one looks at the relatively short time it took to colonize what is now the United States of America, without the advanced technology of today, it is apparent what can be accomplished on the moon and beyond.

This, of course, will open up new horizons and possibilities. Thereafter, the moon will be used as a staging area for further space exploration and population expansion. As I think about the way we have explored and populated the Earth, I can only imagine what our grandchildren will become familiar with. Robotics and computerization are now merging with living physiology to take on new forms of life—a concept that has long been-of interest to me.

The Kabbalah speaks to the development of these issues and more. As a species, we are continually confounded by our quest to understand what life is and will be. As I have stated many times throughout this book, I believe that we are not yet evolutionarily advanced on a sensual level to even begin to comprehend these questions. It seems clear to me that we are advancing by

---

[111]Haridas Chaudhuri, *Being, Evolution and Immortality* (Wheaton, IL: Theosophical Publishing House, 1988).

[112]This theory of progression was advanced by Alvin Toffler in his book *Future Shock* (New York: Random House, 1970). Las Vegas was turned into the mega-entertainment city that it is today out of an area that was previously desolate desert in a period of only seventy to eighty years.

steps on the evolutionary ladder. Those steps are slow, and require patience and time to be understood. A friend shared a metaphor with me to help me to teach my son how to achieve something that requires patience, persistence, and ongoing effort. If one wanted to climb Mt. Everest today, my friend said, that would be almost impossible for most people. However, if one could develop the patience and persistence to build a ramp that only ascended a couple of inches per day, eventually almost anyone could reach the top. Similarly, patience, persistence, imagination, and creativity have to be employed for one to recognize these concepts.

To paraphrase what Sir Arthur Conan Doyle wrote in *Sherlock Holmes*, "When the impossible has been eliminated, all that remains, no matter how improbable, is possible."[113]

We should recognize the theory of evolution, not as an answer to all incomprehensible aspects of the life, but rather as most scientists' best guess, however imperfect, about how we got here in the first place.

Passions run deep about human relationships with the divine. It seems that part of our human frailty is our lack of evolutionary sophistication that would enable us to see the senselessness in the tribal conflicts Protestants versus Catholics, Palestinians versus Israelis, Northerners versus Southerners in the American Civil War, and Christian Crusaders versus Muslims. Yet, the passion of intense beliefs on each side continues to dominate human existence.

At what point in human existence do we become sufficiently evolved to transcend our tribal passions? How can any one of the almost eight billion of us on this planet be the only one to have the right way to commune with the divine? Don't each of us find our path to the divine by virtue of the customs and traditions we were born into? Why must leaders incite the masses through religious passions to further their power base at the expense of others?

After the tragedy of the terrorist acts committed against the World Trade Center on September 11, 2001, Deepak Chopra wrote something poignant about the tribalism of those acts:

> Everything has a cause, so we have to ask, What was the
> root cause of this evil? There is no doubt that such evil is alive

---

[113]The actual quote is, "When you have eliminated the impossible, whatever remains, however improbable, must be the truth." Sir Arthur Conan Doyle, https://en.wikipedia.org/wiki/Sherlock_Holmes/.

all around the world and is even celebrated. Does this evil grow from the suffering and anguish felt by people we don't know and therefore ignore? Have they lived in this condition for a long time? One assumes that whoever did this attack feels implacable hatred for America.

All this hatred and anguish seems to have religion at its basis. Isn't something terribly wrong when jihads and wars develop in the name of God? Isn't God invoked with hatred in Ireland, Sri Lanka, India, Pakistan, Israel, Palestine, and even among the intolerant sects of America?[114]

The most terrifying aspect of the terrorist attack on the twin symbols-of America's financial and military is the abysmal hatred that fueled it. What could be the source of such profound hatred, which motivated nineteen suicidal murderers and those who sent them? The answer is clear: Islamic fundamentalism.

Fundamentalist Islam is the culprit at the present moment, but the correct historical answer is fundamentalist religion in general—especially the supposedly humane monotheistic religions. The fact is that if religious charismatics and clerics insist on their exclusive connection to God, maintaining that they possess the one and only *truth*, sooner or later they will turn bloody, as history bears witness.

If I had lived during many other periods of history, I would have been persecuted, tortured, and eventually killed. At the very least, I would have been ostracized, and probably later burned at the stake for what I have written here.

Myopic beliefs such as those advanced by most organized religions have generally prevailed throughout history—especially in the period following the birth of Jesus. During the preceding periods of paganism, myopic beliefs were held with as much conviction by the masses as are the beliefs today held by religious zealots.

The concept of monotheism was first presented as a divine revelation by Abraham. Ken Kaufman stated, "The new monotheism recounts that there is only one *true* God. The one and *only* true God is an accurate concept. However, the definition of the one and only true God is *your* God ." What

---

[114]Deepak Chopra, *The Deeper Wound* (New York: Harmony Books, 2001).

Ken is saying is that Godliness lies within each of us. Thus, each of is responsible for connecting with the divine and the infinite in a personal way from within. In other words, each of us is a part of the divine. We are each in partnership with creation. Hence the concept of *tikkun olam*.[115]

Isaac Luria, the renowned sixteenth-century Kabbalist, used the phrase *tikkun olam*, usually translated as "repairing the world," to encapsulate the true role of humanity in the ongoing evolution and spiritualization of the cosmos. Luria taught that God created the world by forming vessels to hold the divine light. But as God poured the light into the vessels, they catastrophically shattered, tumbling down toward the realm of matter. Thus, our world consists of countless shards of the original vessels entrapping sparks of the divine light. Humanity's great task involves helping God by freeing and reuniting the scattered light, raising the sparks back to divinity and restoring the broken world.

There are similar concepts in other religions. Jesus exhorted people to prepare for his Second Coming with love. In Buddhism, Bodhisattvas vow to forgo final liberation until all beings have been freed from suffering. The Gnostics held that a spark of divinity resides entrapped within the soul of each human being.

By loving life and by respecting and loving all that is alive, one must realize that we are inextricably connected to everything that has come before. Mother Teresa said, "If we have no peace, it is because we have forgotten that we belong to each other."[116]

We each have our own connection and ability to resonate with the infinite and all of life sources and energies in whatever forms they may take. When we silence our thoughts in order to meditate or pray in any form, we are in fact communing with the infinite—the life force if you will. As a result, we reach a euphoric state, a different level of consciousness that elevates us. There is a saying that "If prayer is when we speak to God, then intuition is when God speaks to us." Historically, then, each of us believes that our path is the correct and only true one. Our prayers then reinforce our beliefs that our religious path must be the one and only correct one.

Therefore, the masses, which have a need to be led and not to question, blindly follow the rituals and mythological interpretations of their spiritual leaders. It is an easy path for them, since it does not require them to ever

---

[115]Available at http://www.innerfrontier.org/Practices/Purification.htm/.
[116]https://en.wikipedia.org/wiki/Mother_Teresa/.

question what they are taught. Their path only requires them to surrender to their absolute faith. Most religions provide answers to spiritual yearnings, making it easy for most people to buy into those answers and adopt them as their own.

Interestingly, one's religion is usually just an accident of birth. Whatever religion or belief system one is born into becomes the base line for one's beliefs. However, advanced spiritual individuals of all belief systems have transcended the myopic constraints and dictates of any one particular path. Instead, they have sought communion with the infinite and divine. They have committed themselves to random acts of kindness toward all living things, realizing that we are all part and parcel of the same life force and energy.

An example of what I am saying may be the teachings of Jesus. I am not referring to the representations of him by people who wrote seventy to ninety years after his death. Such people put their own spin on what he was trying to impart. By the way, his message may very well have been based on Buddhist philosophies that were framed within the context of monotheistic Judaism. It should be noted that there was a period of some twenty to thirty years when Jesus was missing from the historical record. It has been theorized that since his teachings echo in many ways the philosophies of belief systems such as Buddhism, he incorporated those teachings into his practices and philosophies.

If this theory is true, it is hypothesized that Jesus then returned to the Middle East, where he added those beliefs and philosophies to augment the belief system in the Hebrew Bible. He never intended to change one word or letter in what is now referred to by Christians as the "Old Testament." He never represented himself as the son of God, nor did he intend to inspire a "New Testament." To the contrary, he augmented the teachings-of monotheistic Judaism, as well as its rituals and customs, with Eastern beliefs and philosophies. He stated we are all the sons and daughters of God—the God within all of us.

We are all capable of doing similar things. Metaphorically, Jesus washed the feet of others, demonstrating that all God's children deserve being treated in that way. His teachings were never about him. He and never represented himself as anything other than one who had revelations that enabled him to see things in an advanced light. He was a highly evolved spiritual being. His teachings, not the renditions created seventy to ninety years later by Paul and others to further their own agendas, are highly relevant today.

Saul of Tarsus was a Jew who later changed his name to Paul after he converted to Christianity, some seventy to ninety years after the death-of

Jesus. He created his own interpretations of what he thought Jesus had been trying to impart, writing his ideas down based on his own paradigms and myopic views. What he and others wrote, which later came to be called the New Testament, was different from what Jesus was trying to convey.

In creating his own version of the Bible, Thomas Jefferson culled out much of the spin by Paul and the other writers of the New Testament, creating a text that better represents the teachings and wisdom of the man.[117]

The resulting conveyance of Jesus' message has been distorted, and an entirely different spin has been placed on it, by people with their own agendas, bias, and issues. The various councils of men in power ever since have debated and set forth various modified renditions, which enabled the masses. Those members of the masses who did not want to think or were unable to think preferred to follow a prescribed path. That was a means for them to avoid responsibility for their own actions or inactions, thereby absolving themselves of sin by believing that a divinity had given up his life for them. All they had to do was follow the way his teaching had been codified by other men into an organized belief structure, and their path to eternity would be assured. Without that, they would be doomed to eternal damnation.

There is a void within each of us—a longing to be connected, fulfilled, and able to turn to some comprehensible source that can guide us to find solace. We have not yet evolved enough as spiritual beings to discover the answers to those questions that elude us. Those questions remain unanswerable enigmas. Many circumstances in life bring us to our knees at times, rendering us helpless to deal with the reasons for them. They force the weak-minded among us to seek a course of discovery that is easy to follow without questioning. One problem with that approach is that those individuals are left with nowhere to go for resolution within themselves. Thus, as they become aware of their human frailties, they pray to their concept of the almighty. Therefore, they seek resolution from what they believe is an omnipotent entity that can provide that resolution.

In essence, what they are doing is surrounding themselves with what they believe is the source of their existence, based on their tribal traditions.

Have you ever noticed professional athletes who praise their tribal deity—usually Jesus, but sometimes Allah—for their victory? What about the losing athletes? Are they any less connected to the divine?

---

[117] Available at https://en.wikipedia.org/wiki/Jefferson_Bible/.

Wouldn't a more appropriate approach be to commune with the life force that all living things are part of? Shouldn't we be grateful for the ability to be successful, based on preparation, will, and perseverance?

The late Rabbi Lord Jonathan Sacks wrote in *The Great Partnership* about science and religion:

> At various times in history, including now, people have thought that there was a conflict between religion and science. At the time of Galileo, when religion was the stronger of the two, religious belief was used to reject science. Today, when science is stronger, it is sometimes used to reject religion.
>
> In fact, though, this whole idea is mistaken. Religion and science are completely different things, and neither negates the other. They are as unlike as poetry and prose, or song and speech, or a portrait of a person and an MRI scan.
>
> The human mind is capable of doing two quite different things. One is the ability to break things down into their constituent parts and see how they mesh and interact. This is often called "left brain" thinking, and the best example is science. The other, often called "right brain thinking," is the ability to join events together so that they tell a story, or to join people together so that they form relationships. The best example of this is religion.
>
> To put it at its simplest: science takes things apart to see how they work. Religion puts things together to see what they mean. And we need them both, the way we need the two hemispheres of the brain.
>
> Science is about explanation; religion is about interpretation. Science analyzes, religion integrates. Science breaks things down to their component parts; religion binds people together in relationships of trust. Science tells us what is, religion tells us what ought to be. Science describes; religion inspires, beckons, calls.
>
> Science practices detachment: religion is the art of attachment, self to self, soul to soul. Science sees the underlying order of the physical world. Religion hears the music beneath the noise. Science is the conquest of ignorance. Religion is the redemption of solitude.
>
> One way of seeing the difference is to think about their

relationship with time. Science looks for causes of events, and a cause always comes before its effect. How did the window break? Because I threw a stone at it. First came the throwing of the stone, then came the breaking of the window. Science looks back from effect to cause.[118]

Recently, I have been discussing the Kabbalah with my cousin, Renee Cooperman, Ph.D. When I shared the above quote with her, she wrote to me:

There is a lot to consider in this. I have read it over many times. I have never heard the comparison between science and religion laid out quite like this. Science might act like it is trying to remain detached, but of course, science is humble enough to admit that theories and experiments are heavily influenced by the zeitgeist. That is the tension and the struggle for scientists, to try to be objective in the face of an ocean of different limitations like our senses and our "times." But I agree, that's the ideal, to arrive at a truth that is true, no matter who says it or when. "Religion is the redemption of solitude." I think this is a profound point. Mystical experiences that bring on a sense of ecstasy and peace seem to always be described as a sense of connection and oneness with the universe. So, I agree with that observation, too. The ideas of interpretation and integration are not completely unique to religion or absent from science, but I agree, that's the focus and emphasis. But are these two positions different ways of coming to the same conclusion? ...I'll read more and write again. Love, Renee

To continue with the wisdom of Rabbi Lord Jonathon Sacks:

However, human action is always looking forward. Why did I throw the stone? Because I wanted to wake someone who was asleep to warn them that the building next door is on fire.

---

[118]Available at https://rabbisacks.org/great-partnership/.

An action always seeks to bring about something in the future. And that's where religion comes in as our deepest guide to the future: the promised land, the messianic age, the vision of the prophets we travel toward when we work for a world in which people finally recognize the image of God in the people not like them, and so bring an end to violence and war. Or sometimes it's about eternal life and the destiny of the soul after death. Either way, religion isn't about causes but about purposes. Why then do we need science? Because we need to understand the world, if we are to honor God's purposes within it. We need to understand disease if we are to cure it. We need to understand the causes of poverty if we are to alleviate it. We need to understand our destructive drives if we are to rise above them.

And why do we need religion? Because what gives human life its meaning and purpose? The universe is more than the result of an accidental fluctuation in the quantum field at the dawn of time. Human life is more than the unintended consequence of random genetic mutations blindly sifted by natural selection.

Just as there is something within us that is beyond the purely physical, so there is something within the universe—we call it the Divine presence—that is beyond the merely material. And just as God created the universe in love, justice, and compassion, so He calls on us to create relationships of love, justice, and compassion.

Or to put it another way: the difference between religion and science is the difference between the impersonal and the personal.

When you treat impersonal phenomena as if they were persons, the result is myth: light is from the sun God, rain from the sky God, natural disasters from battles between the Gods, and so on. Science was born when people stopped telling stories about nature and instead observed it; in other words, when they relinquished myth.

And when you treat persons impersonally, as if they were objects, the result is dehumanization: people categorized by color, class, or creed and treated differently as a result. The religion of the Bible was born when people stopped seeing people as useful or useless objects and began to see each individual as unique, sacrosanct, the image of God.

So we need both religion and science. Albert Einstein said it most famously: "Science without religion is lame. Religion without science is blind."[119]

We need both: science to understand the universe, and religion to guide our way within it, from the world as it is to the world as it ought to be: a world of peace, justice, compassion, and love, when we, God 's creations, honor God, our Creator.[120]

Human beings' quest for spirituality and connectedness becomes obvious if we merely shed the paradigms cast upon us by our tribal roots. All we need to do to be spiritual is to connect with the Universe and all that was, is, or will be. We need to commune with others, respect life in all its forms, and practice acts of kindness. All of us are in an interactive dance. Hence this poem that I created, entitled "Dance with Me":

Dance with Me

When raindrops fall
and gently caress,
the leaves of trees
the blades of grass.
There are images,
so strong…
Desires,
so innate…
to seek to be sought.
So too the moisture as it seeks the leaf
And glistens innately on the blade
Perfection knows no bounds
nor limits.
Satisfaction although, knows

---

[119] Available at https://en.wikipedia.org/wiki/Albert_Einstein/.
[120] Available at https://rabbisacks.org/great-partnership/.

123

the experience of miraculous moments.
A moment alone
MIRACULOUS,
Yet only the secure may dare.
Moments of connection
MIRACULOUS,
Treasures for all yet
so priceless and rare.
Dance with me as raindrops fall,
but caress my spirit
most of all.

I would like to close this chapter with the stated thought process of Albert Einstein. However, in doing so, I am not stating that his view or the view-of the individual who inspired his view, Baruch Spinoza, are correct. As background, Einstein used many labels to describe his religious views, including "agnostic," "religious nonbeliever," and "pantheistic" believer in "Spinoza's God." Einstein believed that the problem of God was the "most difficult in the world"—a question that could not be answered "simply with yes or no." He conceded that "the problem involved is too vast for our limited minds." Interestingly, this idea is a major premise of the *Zohar*, from the Hebrew זֹהַר, literally "splendor" or "radiance," which is the foundational work in the literature of Jewish mystical thought known as the Kabbalah.[121] The *Zohar* is a group of books that include commentary on the mystical aspects-of the Torah (the five books of Moses). It also contains scriptural interpretations and material on mysticism, mythical cosmogony, and mystical psychology. The *Zohar* contains discussions of the nature of God; the origin and structure of the universe; the nature of souls; redemption; the relationship of Ego to Darkness; and the relationship of "true self" to "The Light of God." Its scriptural exegesis can be considered an esoteric form of the rabbinical literature known as the Midrash, which also elaborates on the Torah.

When Albert Einstein gave lectures at U.S. universities, the recurring question that students asked him most was, Do you believe in God? And he always answered:

---

[121]Available at https://en.wikipedia.org/wiki/Zohar/.

I believe in the God of Baruch de Spinoza.[122]

According to Spinoza: God would say: Stop praying. What I want you to do is go out into the world and enjoy your life. I want you to sing, have fun and enjoy everything I've made for you.

Stop going into those dark, cold temples that you built yourself and saying they are my house. My house is in the mountains, in the woods, rivers, lakes, beaches. That's where I live and there I express my love for you.

Stop blaming me for your miserable life; I never told you there was anything wrong with you or that you were a sinner, or that your sexuality was a bad thing. Sex is a gift I have given you and with which you can express your love, your ecstasy, your joy. So don't blame me for everything they made you believe.

Stop reading alleged sacred scriptures that have nothing to do with me. If you can't read me in a sunrise, in a landscape, in the look of your friends, in your son's eyes... you will find me in no book!

Stop asking me, "Will you tell me how to do my job?" Stop being so scared of me. I do not judge you or criticize you, nor get angry, or bothered. I am pure love.

Stop asking for forgiveness, there's nothing to forgive. If I made you... I filled you with passions, limitations, pleasures, feelings, needs, inconsistencies... free will. How can I blame you if you respond to something I put in you? How can I punish you for being the way you are, if I'm the one who made you? Do you think I could create a place to burn all my children who behave badly for the rest of eternity? What kind of God would do that?

Respect your peers and don't do what you don't want for yourself. All I ask is that you pay attention in your life, that alertness is your guide.

My beloved, this life is not a test, not a step on the way, not a rehearsal, nor a prelude to paradise. This life is the only thing

---

[122]Baruch de Spinoza was a Dutch philosopher considered one of the great rationalists-of seventeenth-century philosophy, along with Descartes.

here and now and it is all you need.

I have set you absolutely free, no prizes or punishments, no sins or virtues, no one carries a marker, no one keeps a record.

You are absolutely free to create in your life. Heaven or hell.

I can't tell you if there's anything after this life, but I can give you a tip. Live as if there is not. As if this is your only chance to enjoy, to love, to exist.

So, if there's nothing after, then you will have enjoyed the opportunity I gave you. And if there is, rest assured that I won't ask if you behaved right or wrong, I'll ask, Did you like it? Did you have fun? What did you enjoy the most? What did you learn...?

Stop believing in me; believing is assuming, guessing, imagining. I don't want you to believe in me, I want you to believe in you. I want you to feel me in you when you kiss your beloved, when you tuck in your little girl, when you caress your dog, when you bathe in the sea.

Stop praising me. What kind of egomaniac God do you think I am?

I'm bored being praised. I'm tired of being thanked. Feeling grateful? Prove it by taking care of yourself, your health, your relationships, the world. Express your joy! That's the way to praise me.

Stop complicating things and repeating as a parakeet what you've been taught about me.

What do you need more miracles for? So many explanations?

The only thing for sure is that you are here, that you are alive, that this world is full of wonders. —Baruch de Spinoza.[123]

---

[123]See at https://en.wikipedia.org/wiki/Religious_and_philosophical_views_of_Albert_Einstein/.

CHAPTER 22

DEALING WITH ADVERSITY

Every adversity carries within it the seed of an equal or greater benefit.

—Napoleon Hill

That which does not kill me will make me stronger.

—Friedrich Nietzsche

Every minute of every day I am getting stronger and stronger in every way.

—Sarah "Sally" Mahr, my mother

These are powerful statements, perhaps much easier to say than to internalize in our lives. When adversity strikes us, our initial reaction is to experience fear, pain, or sorrow. Most of us waste time and energy focusing on regretting what has happened to us. In many instances, we allow ourselves to wallow in the remorseful, stressful depression that adversity deals to us. Although sorrow and grief are part of the process of loss, especially of someone deeply loved, when these feelings are prolonged, they are largely a waste of our time. No matter what the situation is or how severe the depression may be, the famous aphorism "This too shall pass" always applies. The tricky part is what to do while it is passing.

Part of living is experiencing highs and lows, pleasure and pain, good and bad. These characterize the ebb and flow of the whole universe. How much more pleasant and productive our lives would be if we could learn to manage the inevitable adversities we experience throughout life. Instead, we should focus our energy on discovering what benefits await us or what lessons we can learn from experience.

Individuals who recognize adversity as merely "a flat tire on the road of life" are generally more successful than individuals who obsess over their predicament. If, while driving our vehicles, we get waylaid by a flat tire, we naturally take action by either changing the tire ourselves with a spare or calling a road service to change the tire for us. Then we make arrangements to get a new tire. More serious adversity is no different. We have to take action and get on with our lives. No matter what the adversity is, it is not an end point, but rather a chance for a new beginning. Perhaps it will take us in a different direction than we planned, but nevertheless we must stay the course of our lives.

An example of such resilience is the late actor Christopher Reeves, who, at the height of his career, was stopped short by an almost fatal accident while riding a horse. He went from a vital, mobile, handsome man at the top of his game to a quadriplegic confined to a wheelchair and life-support systems. Yet, the whole world was captivated when they saw him on the broadcast of the Academy Awards, delivering a message for health and humanitarian causes to which he had now dedicated his life. Reeves was a survivor. He exemplified the affirmation that "it is not what happens to me that matters, but how I *deal* with what happens to me."

Over the course of my career, I used to tell the members of my staff, "We don't have problems; rather, we have opportunities with varying degrees of difficulty." How we are judged by our performance during adversity is not unlike a diving competition in which the various dives are rated according to their degree of difficulty. How many of us are expecting a score of tens across the board? Success rarely comes to those who don't expect it.

To cope with adversity, stay busy, productive, and occupied. Perhaps even try to help others to overcome their adversities. Dorothea Brande, in *Wake Up and Live*, wrote: "All that is necessary to break the spell of frustration and inertia is to act as if it is impossible to fail."[124] Failure is not an option. You must proceed as if limits to your ability do not exist. If need be, "Fake it until you make it."

A pathway to happiness and success is self-discipline and persistence—in

---

[124]Available at https://en.wikipedia.org/wiki/Dorothea_Brande/.

other words, attaining an "Iron Will." We must not allow ourselves to be thrown off course by the many distractions and adversities that life presents to us. We can mitigate the negative impact of adversity by maintaining the right attitude, taking immediate action, and remaining on course. We need to take life one day at a time. Perhaps the most beneficial of all affirmations for dealing with adversity is stated in the Serenity Prayer: "God grant me the serenity to accept the things I cannot change, the courage to change the things I can, and the wisdom to know the difference."

For every second of every day of our existence, we have choices. The choices we make at any given instant determine a sequence of events that may not otherwise unfold for us. When one is on a journey and comes to a fork in the road, the sights, encounters, obstacles, and events that one experiences are obviously different from those presented by the other fork.

So what about those choices? Why do we make them? What motivates us to select one over another? How much due diligence do we perform? Do we analyze the potentialities of our choices? Are we disciplined and calculated, or emotional and impulsive?

If we judge our performances based on our fantasies of what they should be or on the perceived successes of others, we sentence ourselves to unhappiness and lack of fulfillment. Perhaps our conclusion that we are unable to compete with those fantasies or perceptions causes us to sabotage our efforts, leading us to mediocrity or a string of failures.

Figure 19: Mathew Schwartz Unsplash

129

CHAPTER 23

DEATH

A part of living is dying.

—F. Sanford Mahr

if you so choose

if you so choose
to remember me
please not with a tear....
rather
reflect upon
what's been said and done
for those encountered
those held dear...
a daughter, a son.
know well
the place to seek
its secret revealed
since taught awareness
of their heart's beat
a friend.... a comrade
in arms or not
can recall
the words
the acts
the matter of facts....

if you so choose
to remember me
please not with a tear....
rather ...,
laugh;
love;
dance;
sing;
create;
seek resonance with life;
facilitate
it is now that matters
not then
not to be
if you so choose
so remember me

My writing about death can be best served by inserting a letter I wrote to Jerry Faitelson, one of my closest friends, when he experienced the loss of his mother. That letter best expresses my opinions on the subject. I have omitted the names.

My Dearest Friend,

I know you are, of course, experiencing a plethora of feelings now, which is quite to be expected. I have been thinking about you on a fairly regular basis, especially since your mother's passing.

Whenever I have thoughts of you, there is, of course, the wondering of how you are, yet knowing without asking how you must be. Although not so much time has passed since your loss, I imagine, with time's passing, fewer people are now in contact with you; and although I am sure that you are still supported by your closest friends and family, nevertheless, based on my own experiences, I know that the void must still be tremendous, the pain and sorrow deep as they come and go.

It is difficult for others to offer solace to someone in the throes of grief. Most have no idea what to do to offer comfort, or something more useful than condolences and expressions of "I'm so sorry." Although the sympathy, support, and sentiment are certainly appreciated and well-intended, their usefulness is most often marginal.

I remember a speech that President Reagan gave to the families of U.S. servicemen who had unexpectedly died in a plane crash. He told each of the family members that he was deeply saddened at their loss, and in an impeccable speech went on to remind them of "the joy it was to have known those fine young men and women, the joy it was to witness the things they said and the jokes they played, the kindness they did and how they laughed." President Reagan then said something very important. It was important because bereaved people have a tendency to punish themselves with extra anguish by regretting words unsaid, or actions not taken, or little extra gestures of affection they wish weren't withheld. He said, "Think for a moment of the joy you gave them and be glad."

I know there were many words expressed and stories told, from the countless number of people that your beloved mother touched throughout her ever so meaningful life. I can only begin to imagine the treasure of memories you must have experienced with her. Everyone that interacted with her was affected by her being in some way. What a special person she was.

So few people are spared the agony of losing someone profoundly loved. I sincerely believe and have learned from my own experiences that concentration in a time of grief, not only on the virtues of the person loved and lost, but also on the love and joy we gave them, helps to some degree to calm the pain. It is with that in mind that I share the following with you, with the sincere hope that you might glean some benefit from hearing about this and perhaps be able to apply some things to what you are going through.

When I was a young man, in my very early twenties, my father was murdered. He was 57 at the time. Three years later, my mother died; she was only 56. I remember all too well, even to this day, the events as they unfolded—seemingly with a life of their own, at a pace that was at times much too fast and other times much too slow. At times, it was just like being a spectator observing a nightmare that would never end. At other times, it was like being a participant in the worst of all possible dreams. There was the seemingly never ending parade of people horrified at my father's senseless murder. Yet, for the most part, they were at a loss as to how to truly comfort my mother and her children. Yet, people were always there, and even though we all wanted to be alone in our grief and sorrow, in the beginning they were there anyway. Retrospectively, I now am thankful that they were there, and thankful also that our religion has the traditions of mourning that it does, to help us cope with the horrific experience.

After my father's murder, my mother took some small comfort in observing the utmost traditional Jewish mourning traditions, and my brother, sister, and I did it along with her at her insistence. First, the shiva, then the thirty-day period after, called Shloshim, and then going to Temple with her for the next eleven months, so that she could say Kaddish. It worked for her and helped her deal with her pain and loss. It was different for each of us, though; as I am sure it is and will be for you and your family. I remember looking everywhere for something from my father. Some instructions, a sign, anything, one last contact, maybe a chance to say the things I never had a chance to say to him. Alternatively, perhaps just to find out from him what to do, as I was now the "head of the family." I can remember lying in bed some nights and saying to myself, "Listen, Dad, I know you're dead, but if I could just call you for a minute, just one word, anything, please." Of course, there was nothing, only the pain, and sometimes the sobering albeit slight memories of things he had said or done.

My mother and he were so much in love and had such a close relationship that she could hardly cope after he was gone. She would lie in bed, night after night, crying his name, while my brother and I, who had moved back in with her, were beside ourselves with trying to figure out what to do for her, let alone come to terms with our own sorrow and loss.

Eventually, we found some purpose and tried to make some meaning out of the senselessness of it all by starting a campaign in New York State to have gun control laws enacted that would make it a mandatory jail sentence for anyone using a gun to commit a crime, in addition to the penalty for the crime. That effort—which was successful, by the way—did prove to offer us all a purpose and a means of going on. My mother's activity helped her to some degree as well. Then, just when things seemed to get a little more bearable, at least for my brother, sister, and me, she suddenly died. Actually, she died in my brother's arms while he was trying to revive her from a heart attack that was apparently induced by her choking on a cookie. It was unbelievable. My brother was traumatized. A young kid of 20, who in his mind failed to save his mother from dying, and, prior to that, a 17-year-old who saw our father lying murdered in the parking lot of his drugstore.

I was just a 24-year-old at that time, and although I was somewhat hardened after my father's murder, I was still traumatized. I literally had no one to go to for direction or support. Sure, there were extended family members and friends, but ultimately everything was left up to me to take charge and try to make some sense of it all. I had to face my own loss, fear, guilt, and grief, and then help my family members to try to carry on in whatever ways I could. I had to find the strength myself to do that. No one else could do it for me. Where the strength came from I don't know to this day, but eventually it came.

Although none of what I have shared with you can possibly compare with what you have experienced and must still be experiencing, nevertheless a loss is a loss. I guess there are varying degrees of loss, but regardless of degree, each carries with it an indescribable emptiness and pain that can only be partially related to by people who have had similar experiences.

I will spare you all of the unfathomable details of my brother's death only a few years ago and the emotional roller coaster that involved. Suffice it to say that my brother's attempt to save my mother with CPR went full circle as I tried unsuccessfully to save him at our uncle's funeral when he collapsed while giving a eulogy, many years later. I mention this only because I care about what you are going through and feel deeply for your loss. I thought that perhaps hearing of these experiences might in some small way offer you something, I am not even sure what.

I want to reiterate that I have learned a lot about loss, and life and death, through all my experiences—none of which came right away or I even wanted to learn or know about. In a strange way, it was easier just to experience the deep pain and sorrow, rather than strive to go on.

Eventually, I took comfort in remembering and in trying to live my life in the manner I thought my father and mother would have wanted, albeit making many mistakes along the way. It was and is to this day helpful to remember them, the things they taught me, the little funny things they did and that we all experienced together as a family. At first, I shied away from doing things that reminded me of the experiences we had shared together. At first, I shuddered at hearing the stories about them from others. All that did was remind me of my parents not being there anymore. It hurt and I was scared to keep being reminded. Later, I learned that remembering them, the good things, the good times, and hearing about things they did that had positive impacts on others, was really where the healing occurred. I hope with all of my heart that you will find that place, too.

I have learned that time is healing, but it does not "heal all wounds," as the saying goes. Life and the multiverse do not work according to what we think should be. Rather, there are random happenstances that we are all subjected to and are forced to learn to live with. That is just the way it is.

I have learned that death is so hard for those of us who remain, because we are not yet evolved enough to comprehend the passing of life from physical to spiritual. Yet, by studying the Kabbalah, I have learned that for those who are or were aware of the multidimensional universe that we are a part of, that they have no fear of death, no sorrow at experiencing it, save for the loss of physical contact with those they love and miss. The famous Psalm number 23 by King David speaks to this: "Though I walk through the valley of the shadow of death, I will fear no evil, for thou art with me." Apparently, King David was one of those rare few humans who were evolved enough to understand.

I have learned in a very painful way that reading, listening, remembering, and studying have helped to allow me to gain a better understanding of life, death, and loss. Those activities allowed me to transcend what life has presented to me. Once again, it is not my intention to impose on you what worked for me. However, I am sharing my thoughts with you in the hope that some of them will resonate with you.

Regardless of their own experiences, no one can really understand what you are feeling. There really are no words of comfort, no actions or lack of actions that can placate the emptiness, hurt, and sorrow that you must feel.

Years ago, when I was the president of the Tampa Jewish Federation, Harold Kushner, the author of *When Bad Things Happen to Good People*,[125] was in Tampa, speaking at a community dinner function. During dinner, he told me, "The most effective thing a person can do for someone during their period of grief is to hold their hand and be with them, rather than try to offer reasons, explanations, and words of condolence." This letter is my little way of trying to hold your hand and be with you, my friend.

Take whatever comfort you can from the life your beloved mother led and the legacy she left behind for you and future generations. Death is not an end but a beginning for the soul of the person that has passed. You, of course, realize that the only pain is the pain felt by those who have been left behind, not by the one who has passed. Actually, your beloved mother is finally out of pain, embarking on a great new adventure. She is once again a spirit continuing its journey. The soul that you knew as your beloved mother has transcended to another level. What she believed in as a mother, wife, friend, relative, community member, and giver to all will, of course, live on through you, those whom she touched, and those whom you will touch with her ways going forward. As I wrote in one of my poems, "There are those she touched, there are those they touched, and there are those yet to be touched."

Remember the good things, remember the lessons, the

---

[125]Harold S. Kushner, *When Bad Things Happen to Good People* (New York: Schocken Books, 1981).

challenges, laugh at the funny moments, and continue the celebration of life as she clearly would want you to do.

From the times I saw her, or from viewing photographs of her, I recall the joy and sparkle in her eyes as she was with you and her family and friends. You made her more than proud. What more can anyone want or expect from life?

I have learned at great emotional expense not to hold back tears, but also not to hold back smiles and pleasant thoughts, either. One does not need to be strong and brave, and thereby sublimate one's emotions, which will come and go as waves. Nevertheless, I hope you will celebrate the amazing opportunity you have been given as the son of a wonderful exceptional woman who, without doubt, loved you very much.

The following are words of wisdom that were spoken by The Rebbe,[126] among various others of his teachings that Simon Jacobson assembled in his book *Toward a Meaningful Life: The Wisdom of the Rebbe Menachem Mendel Schneerson.*[127]

What Does Death Really Mean?

Death is the elevation of the soul to a more sublime existence.

The mystery of death is part of the enigma of the soul and life itself; understanding death really means understanding life. During life as we know it, the body is vitalized by the soul; upon death there is a separation between body and soul.

Modern physics has taught that no substance truly disappears, that it only changes form, that matter is another form of energy.

---

[126]Available at https://en.wikipedia.org/wiki/Menachem_Mendel_Schneerson/.

[127]Simon Jacobson, *The Wisdom of The Rebbe Menachem Mendel Schneerson* (New York: William Morrow, 1995).

The spiritual life force in man, the soul, never disappears; upon death, it changes from one form to another, higher form.

Before we can truly answer the question "What is death?" we need to first ask "What is life?" By medical definition, life takes place when one's brain and heart are functioning. Yet, a person can be biologically alive, but not alive at all; breathing and walking and talking are only manifestations of what we call life. The true source of life, the energy that allows the body to function, is the soul. And the soul is immortal. While the manifestations of life may cease upon death, the soul lives on, only in a different form.

The soul is fueled by the inexhaustible energy of the good deeds a person performed on Earth, and it lives on materially through his or her children and the others who perpetuate his or her spiritual vitality.

For those who continue to look at only the outer layer of life, the physical component as circumscribed by the human body, death indeed seems to be the end of life. But we must learn to peer inside this outer layer and see the human soul, our connection to eternity.

Very sincerely and with caring,
Your Friend,
F. Sanford Mahr

> *"Time," the Captain said, "is not what you think." He sat down next to Eddie. "Dying? Not the end of everything. We think it is. But what happens on Earth is only the beginning."*

> —Mitch Albom[128]

---

[128] Available at https://en.wikipedia.org/wiki/Mitch_Albom/.

SOME PARTING THOUGHTS

Be careful of being judgmental of those you meet, for they are all facing hard battles and issues not unlike those that you are facing.

—Plato

Past glories make for poor feeding.

—Isaac Asimov

Writing this book has been an enlightening, enjoyable, and educational experience. The process of writing and compiling has taken me on a journey of learning and growth over many years. It has been interesting to me to see the different perspectives on each of the topics I have addressed, and how my thoughts have evolved over time, and will continue to evolve.

Although I intended the topics I covered in this book to be comprehensive, and hopefully relevant to my readers, perhaps I could have included other subjects as well—such as "Understanding, Patience, and Compassion," "Goal Setting," and "Recreation, Relaxation, and Play."

Some of the chapters in this book are longer than others, but that was not intended to place greater emphasis on some subjects more than others.

After rereading these pages in preparation for these closing comments, I realized that all of the words, concepts, knowledge, and references to other authors mean very little if they do not lead to action. How many of us can talk the talk, but are unable to walk the walk? It is time not merely to *know*, but to *do*. The bottom line of creation in life is doing! We must all be proactive, not reactive! We must all aim for high levels of achievement. As my father used to say, "Son, it is only crowded and competitive at the bottom and middle of any endeavor. The top remains wide open." We must apply what the sage Hillel said: "If I am not for myself, who will be for me? If I am only for myself, what good am I? If not *now*, when?"

T. E. Lawrence wrote in his memoirs:

All people dream, but not all equally. Those who dream by night in the dusty recesses of their minds wake in the day to find it was only vanity; but the dreamers of the day are dangerous, for they may act their dreams with open eyes, and make them possible.[129]

Calvin Coolidge once said:

Nothing in the world can take the place of persistence. Talent will not; nothing is more common than unsuccessful men with talent. Genius will not; unrecorded genius is almost a proverb. Education will not; the world is full of educated derelicts. Persistence and determination alone are omnipotent.[130]

As I stated early in the Introduction to this book, on the night before I left home in my early twenties to become a professional musician, my father taped this note to my bedroom door:

Today is a new day. What will you have, success or failure? The choice is yours and only yours. It is up to you. What you are and what you become will be determined by what you do today. Once today is lost, it is lost forever, never to return. Choose success, and you will be happier, son. Do the right thing. You know what it is.

BE | DO | HAVE
Be — We Are
Do — We Create
Have — We Produce

---

[129] Available at https://en.wikiquote.org/wiki/T._E._Lawrence/.
[130] Available at https://en.wikipedia.org/wiki/Calvin_Coolidge/.

Roots never get the appreciation that a flower does, but that doesn't make them envious.[131]

—Debasish Mridha

The fifteen selections included in this Appendix have been chosen from among my papers and collection of writings. They are included to provide real examples that illustrate various areas of the living of life and achieving excellence. Each selection in the Appendix is offered as a metaphoric navigation, or a compass if you will, to use as a guide through some of the experiences and challenges of life you may encounter or have already encountered:

- A Gentleman's Creed
- Notes to My Daughter
- A Medical Odyssey – Survival and Recovery
- Back in The Day – Interview by Rachael Mahr 2001
- FSM Birthday Letter – My Mother's Tree
- Brushstrokes on the Landscape of Life
- Be Grateful and Proactive
- Eulogy for My Brother
- Birthday Message to My Brother, Eric Aryeh Mahr z'l
- Thanksgiving Is Not a Day, It is a Way
- To Be a Warrior
- One Warrior's Recollections
- This Too Shall Pass: FSM Letter to RHG with poem following
- Eagles and Ducks
- The Good Morning Sun

---

[131]Available at https://www.quotes.wiki/tag/debasish-mridha/.

A GENTLEMAN'S CREED

_____

Created for my son, Andrew Jacob Mahr, 1997

At all times, in every situation, and in every circumstance, *always* be a Gentleman.

Always ask yourself before taking an action, or when interacting with someone, or when confronted with a situation: "Is what I am about to do, or the way I am about to act, what a Gentleman would do?" Or: "How can I handle this as a Gentleman should?"

A Gentleman *always* acts with *honor* and according to his own self-imposed code of conduct.

A Gentleman knows that there are only two ways to do something or act: the *right way* and the *wrong way*. A Gentleman *always* tries to do things and act the *right way*.

A Gentleman *always* maintains eye contact and a firm handshake.

A Gentleman is *always* kind, courteous, and respectful.

A Gentleman knows that civility is a sign of strength, not weakness.

A Gentleman speaks softly and authoritatively, although at times humbly.

A Gentleman knows that saving face is important and *always* gives his opponent or adversary the opportunity to withdraw.

A Gentleman is positive, upbeat, and knows that his attitude is more important than his aptitude.

A Gentleman knows that mutual respect is the key to avoiding conflict.

A Gentleman *always* listens attentively and does not interrupt.

A Gentleman smiles frequently. He knows that the shortest

distance between any two people is a smile.

A Gentleman *always* treats a woman or girl graciously, with respect, and in a chivalrous manner.

A Gentleman *always* defends a woman's or girl's honor and realizes that although women and girls are men's equals and should always be respected as such, they are also *special* and deserve treated as special.

A Gentleman *always* is respectful of his elders.

A Gentleman's word is *always* his bond.

A Gentleman tries to learn something from everyone he meets.

A Gentleman knows how to disagree without being disagreeable.

A Gentleman is *never* judgmental when he disagrees with others.

A Gentleman accepts people for who they are and what they are—understanding that all people have a right to believe in whatever they choose, so long as it doesn't harm others.

A Gentleman's policy is "Honesty is the *only* policy."

A Gentleman *always* seeks first to understand before being understood.

A Gentleman is understated and knows that being and having are what matter. A Gentleman does not talk about what he has or is; he just has it or is it.

A Gentleman knows that it is not only what good we do that matters, but perhaps of greater importance is to realize that it is the good that we *fail* to do that matters most in the long run.

A Gentleman seeks excellence in all things and endeavors.

A Gentleman *always* strives to accomplish more than his best, thereby reaching for at least 1% over 100%.

A Gentleman respects nature and other people's property and possessions.

A Gentleman *never* takes unfair advantage of anyone or anything.

A Gentleman maintains a commitment to Constant and Never-Ending Improvement (C.A.N.E.I.) in all things and every aspect of his life.

A FEW RULES FOR MY DAUGHTER, RACHAEL SARAH MAHR

(as inspired by the author's friend, Raphael Ruiz)

• Travel light through life. Keep only what you need.
• It's okay to cry when you're hurt. It's also okay to smash (some) things; but wash your face, clean your mess, and get up off the floor when you're done. You don't belong down there.
• If you're going to curse, be clever. If you're going to curse in public, know your audience.
• Seek out the people and places that resonate with your soul.
• Just because you can, doesn't mean you should.
• Five-second rule: It's just dirt. There are worse things in a fast-food cheeseburger..
• Happiness is not a permanent state. Wholeness is. Don't confuse them.
• Never walk through an alley alone.
• Be less sugar, more spice, and only as nice as you're able to be without compromising yourself.
• *Can't* is a cop-out.
• Hold your heroes to a high standard. Be your own hero.
• If you can't smile with your eyes, don't smile at all. Insincerity is nothing to aspire to.
• Never lie to yourself.
• Your body, your rules.
• If you have an opinion, you should know why.
• Practice your passions.
• Ask for what you want. The worst thing they can say is no.
• Wish on stars and dandelions, then get to work to make your wishes happen.

- Stay as sweet as you are.
- Fall in love often—particularly with ideas, art, music, literature, and far-off places.
- Say "Please," "Thank you," and "Pardon me" whenever the situation warrants it.
- Reserve "I'm sorry" for when you truly are.
- Naps are for grown-ups, too.
- Question everything except your own intuition.
- You have enough. You *are* enough.
- You are amazing! Don't let anyone ever make you feel you are not. If someone does, walk away. You deserve better.
- Always remember, no matter where you are, you can always come home.
- Be happy and remember your roots. Family is *everything*.
- Say what you mean, and mean what you say.
- Be kind; treat others the way you would like them to treat you.
- Whenever you are in doubt, remember whose daughter you are, and straighten your crown.

A MEDICAL ODYSSEY
survivalandrecovery.blogspot.com/

This journey began before the actual event.

by F. Sanford Mahr

The doctors all told me that one of the reasons I survived the medical odyssey described here and one of the main things that helped to save my life was that I was in such good physical condition from exercise and good nutrition for years before this happened.[132]

Our scars have the power to remind us that our past was real.

—Hannibal Lecter[133]

F ebruary 18, 2000, began as a typical day in my life. It started with a breakfast meeting at the Tampa Club with the then acting Dean of the University of Tampa College of Business and various other appointed committee members.[134] We were interviewing one of the candidates for the position of Dean of the College of Business.

---

[132]This writing is also published online at http://survivalandrecovery.blogspot.com/.

[133]A line spoken by Anthony Hopkins in the film *Red Dragon*.

[134]For many years, I was a member of the Dean's Advisory Council for the College of Business at the University of Tampa.

One of my fellow committee members was a well-known, highly successful woman whom I enjoyed meeting.[135] The breakfast meeting lasted approximately an hour and a half, after which I went back to my office to act on a full calendar of calls, appointments, and various other business activities. My plans were to end the day with my regular workout[136] at The Harbor Island Athletic Club, followed by an evening with a woman I had been dating for a few weeks.

During an appointment around noon for a project I was marketing,[137] I wasn't feeling exactly myself, although I wasn't sure what was wrong. By early afternoon, it was becoming clearer and clearer to me that something serious was not right, so I cancelled an appointment with a good friend of mine, Norman Linton, and an environmental engineer to look at a property that Norman was considering acquiring. I remained in my office and completed business calls and other activities, although at a somewhat slower pace than usual.

During the last call that I intended to make before going to the athletic club, I got into an argument with a long-standing client over a discrepancy of $4,000 that he owed me in fees. I was infuriated because this was a pattern with this client, and the last time it had happened, he had promised me that it would never happen again. While I was talking to him, I was feeling sicker and sicker, and just knew that I had to get off the phone.

A little later, while I was still at my desk, I suddenly felt a sharp intense pain in my neck. The best way I can describe it is that it felt like wooden pencils were stabbing my throat, which took my breath away. When my heart started beating faster and palpitating, I lay my head down on my desk, hoping for some relief. However, when that didn't help, I went to the bathroom, splashed cold water on my face, and lay down in one of the nearby bedrooms. But that still brought no relief.

At that point, I knew that whatever was happening had to be serious, so I

---

[135]This woman, who was part of a company that went public, also had investments in a women's clothing store and purchased some of the dresses that had belonged to Princess Diana. After Princess Di's death, this woman gained worldwide recognition by donating some of the dresses to benefit Princess Di's causes.

[136]For most weeks, I worked out every day, but at least for five days per week, for one and a half to two hours, with a combined and varied exercise regimen of weights and cardiovascular routines.

[137]The meeting was with my friend Brian and a real estate broker who represented Amsouth Bank, a prospective tenant.

decided to drive myself to an emergency room. First, though, I checked my health insurance file to make sure to go to a hospital where my insurance policy offered maximum coverage. Thankfully, as it turned out, that hospital, St. Joseph's, also had the best heart surgery department in the area, although it was by no means the closest hospital. Along the way, I called my friend, Dr. Steve Kreitzer, and left a message with his answering service.

The hospital admitted me immediately, and fortunately the emergency room doctor there had the good sense to administer something to me for the pain and something to lower my blood pressure. Steve Kreitzer was not on call, but his new associate, Adam Katz, was covering for him. Adam didn't know me at all, and at first didn't know what was wrong with me. He may have been somewhat put off by me, since I was being a bit belligerent, thanks to my pain and fears. I am sure I was very demanding and difficult. However, Adam was instrumental in assisting with the eventual diagnosis. It was because of him that an echocardiogram was ordered.

After ruling out various possibilities following the echocardiogram, the doctors performed a CT scan of my chest. Then they consulted a prominent cardiovascular surgeon, Dr. Enrique Lopez, who knew of me from the days when I had been chairman of the Board of Directors of the American Heart Association in Tampa Bay. Dr. Lopez informed me that I had a very serious condition, known as a dissection of the ascending thoracic aorta. After advising me of the high risks involved, he told me I had no choice but immediate emergency surgery. The alternative, he said, was that I would most likely die. Later, I learned that 92 percent of the people who have that surgery in an emergency die on the operating table.

I called my ex-wife, Carol, who was living in Maryland with our two children and her second husband, explained what was going on, and asked to talk to my son and daughter, who were respectively 11 and 14 at the time. Carol was sympathetic and immediately went to pick up our children at their various activities, so we could talk before I went into surgery. It was difficult for me to hear their voices, for they were trying so hard to be strong for me and to hold back their tears. I tried to hold mine back as well.

"Everything will be fine," I said. "I'll see you soon."

I knew they would be coming down to Tampa, but I honestly wasn't sure I would ever see them again. I can only imagine how frightened they must have been. I was already very heavily sedated and scared, but I still had the sense to speak briefly with my sister, Marilyn, who was in Fort Lauderdale.

"I think it might be a good idea if you come over here," I said.

I also had a nurse call some of my friends—Neil Cantor, Richard Gorbaty, and Norman Linton—to tell them what was going on and to provide them with the names and phone numbers of key people I was working with on various projects and other matters that I deemed important. I even asked Neil to stay in touch with those people and keep them in the loop while I was going through this emergency, and he did that in his usually thorough and dependable way.

Although I was drugged, I asked Norman Linton to please handle a couple of financial matters for me, which I had intended to take care of after the weekend. He did that for me, and even went beyond that by helping my family financially throughout my ordeal.

My sister called my brother, Eric, who was living in Israel, although I didn't get to speak to him at that time. I do remember, however, hearing his voice when I eventually woke up from the surgery. After the voices of my children, his voice had the most significance for me.

When Steve Kreitzer called me, just before I went into surgery, he reassured me how necessary it was, and that I would get premier care with Dr. Lopez as the lead surgeon.

The next thing I remember was seeing Dr. Lopez, who had a calming, reassuring, and comforting manner.

After that, I was placed on a gurney, where I was prepared for the surgery.

The last person I remember seeing was Norman Linton's girlfriend at that time, Connie Wickstrand, who came with Norman to the hospital right after I talked to him on the phone. Connie held my hand in a gentle compassionate way as I was wheeled off to the surgical theater. Her kindness was comforting and took my loneliness and some of my fear away.

In my drugged state, I said to her, "There's nothing like a mother's touch, is there? Thank you for sharing your motherly touch."

Then, with a whoosh of the wheels under the gurney, I saw the bright lights of the hospital corridor ceiling passing by like a blur of headlights on a heavily trafficked road in the dark of night. The lights were anonymous and blurred, illuminating me as I was transported to the even brighter, colder, and more sterile-looking operating room.

There was activity all around, with lots of people doing lots of different things. But despite their presence, the room felt empty, for I was very cold, very alone, and very scared. As I lay under all the bright lights, I sensed the intense mood among the doctors, nurses, and technicians. They were all totally focused on the details of their tasks at hand, and not one of them was at all interested in my meager attempts at humor.

When the anesthesiologist came over to me, I was hazy, but I remember that he looked powerful, and the light behind him illuminated him in a way that made him stand out from everyone else.

"Is this it?" I asked. "If so, please make the drugs strong and good."

That's the last thing I remember.

Four weeks later, I woke up, unable to speak or breathe on my own. I couldn't even write legibly. Everyone told me that it was a miracle I had even survived. As a matter of fact, one of the members of the surgical team visited me in my hospital room after I was out of the ICU, and confided to me how lucky I really was. He said that he and his team had difficulties getting my heart and lungs to function again after the surgery, and they had to resort to using a defibrillator numerous times.

My sister Marilyn flew in from Ft. Lauderdale and took charge, the best she could, of keeping everyone informed and insulating me from all the well-wishers who wanted to see me while I was in the Cardiac Intensive Care Unit.

My brother Eric flew in from Israel and spent weeks at my side. He advocated for me with the doctors and made various logistical decisions. In order for him to be able to observe the Sabbath, for he was an Orthodox Jew, kosher food was brought to him, and he even slept in the waiting room of the ICU, so he wouldn't have to drive. When he couldn't be with me at the hospital, he was on the phone with me multiple times each day and totally involved in every aspect of what was going on.

My sister and her then boyfriend ended up staying at my home for more than a month. Together with my brother, Neil Cantor, and Norman Linton, they kept everything on track. What an awesome amount of love and caring they all provided.

Richard Gorbaty did not let the hospital get away with providing anything less than the best service, even though my health insurance company made that difficult. Neil Cantor handled matters on both a business and personal level. Norman Linton even gave money to my family members for their own use, without expecting to be repaid. My children were there, and my ex-wife came as well, along with some of her local girlfriends, who were there to support her. Many other friends and caring family members brought an outpouring of loving concern and provided support, each in their own way.

As for me, I was in a coma, oblivious to everything that was going on—heavily sedated and connected to life-support systems and various other machines. Unconscious, I was hanging on, but it was only the life-support systems, the medications, the constant professional care, and the prayers, love, and support of family members and friends that kept me alive.

There were many complications and issues at various points. The doctors told my family that they didn't know what the outcome would be. It was a day-to-day vigil. My friend, doctor, and fellow synagogue congregant, Steve Kreitzer, even told our rabbi that it was not a good situation and could go either way. I had a tracheotomy, was connected to a respirator, was on a catheter, and received nutrition only through a feeding tube that was inserted through my left nostril and channeled all the way down to my stomach. Oxygen was being pumped into me. Pain medications were provided by means of IV's and direct lines. Additional medications to control my heart rate and my blood pressure were also provided. The doctors gave me various antibiotics to combat infections and the resulting fevers. At various points, my temperature rose as high as 105 degrees. Diuretics were used to address the accumulation of fluids in my lungs and pericardial sac.

I was placed on a special bed, thanks to the intervention of my friend Richard Gorbaty, who advocated for it, even though the hospital said it wasn't covered by my insurance policy. He was adamant and insisted, so the hospital finally provided it. The bed rose, turned, and put my body through movement that it was unable to do on its own. The bed could also lower its temperature in order to deal with my intense fevers. Throughout this process, I lost a great deal of blood.

Apparently, as I learned much later, the rabbi at my temple mentioned my condition during services and my need for blood, after which many of my family members and friends donated blood on my behalf, including my ex-wife Carol, Richard Gorbaty, Kevin Cohen, and many others.

Further complications ensued, starting with pneumonia. My left lung collapsed, half of my diaphragm was paralyzed, and I had encephalopathy of the brain. On top of all that, as they told me weeks after I was home, I had a mini-stroke, which is one of the many risks from this type of surgery. Fortunately, as they later told me, I was lucky that the stroke occurred in a portion of my brain that does not affect speech, movement, and so many other things that could have easily been affected. There is no telling what the result might have been if the particles of blood clotting and other material that lined the inside of my aorta had shot up to my brain through my carotid arteries to another section of my brain.

There is little I remember about the weeks I lay comatose in the Cardiac Intensive Care Unit. Perhaps that was a blessing, since I had been kissed by death. As is written in the *Zohar*, "The Book of Splendor," one of the literary works of the Kabbalah, "a kiss is the merging of one breath with another." However, in this instance, death's kiss was intent on taking my breath away. But it was not to prevail. All I remember, and I can still recall it with vivid detail, was being in tremendous pain, being colder than I had ever been, and being so very tired. I had the sense that the pain, the cold, and the fatigue would never go away.

But I do remember that I had a pervasive sense, an intuition if you will, that if I could just move my body to a place that I saw clearly in my mind, the pain, the cold, and the fatigue would end. I tried to go there, but to no avail. It was an undefined place—very dark, pitch black, and without shape or form. I couldn't get to it, though. I tried and tried and tried. But no matter how hard I tried, I couldn't move from where I was. I was getting colder and colder, in more and more pain, and more tired than ever—so tired that I couldn't move. I even tried to crawl to that special place. I literally visualized dragging myself there on my hands and knees. Finally, after an enormous amount of futile effort, I started to inch my way there. Ever so slowly, with persistence, I was getting there. The closer I got, the more the cold and pain seemed to lessen, and I could relax. I could feel myself getting closer and closer. All I could think about was, *At last, I can rest.*

When I was almost there, I suddenly heard faint voices saying sweetly, "I love you, Daddy," and then, in a deeper tone, "You are the best, Dad."

It was my children, Rachael and Andrew.

I wanted to go to them. I didn't care about the cold, the pain, or the fatigue. I tried to stop crawling to the imaginary place, but I couldn't. A magnetic force seemed to be pulling me closer and closer to it. I tried to stand up, but was unable to. I felt stuck, as if quicksand were sucking me in deeper and deeper.

Then the voices became louder and louder.

"I love you, Daddy" in a soft sweet tone, and then, "You're the best, Dad" in a deeper tone.

With a surge of all the effort I could muster, I thrust myself toward the voices. When I opened my eyes, Rachael and Andrew were standing by my bed, saying those very words.

That is when the doctors say I came out of the coma. It was at that point that I started to turn my situation around. The fever that had been so worrisome started to break. Later, I learned that the doctors had told my family that they had done everything for me that they could. I was either going to come out of it and respond within the next twenty-four hours—or not.

My family members and closest friends had been coming in to the ICU during the twenty-minute intervals they were allowed every hour, maintaining a constant vigil, continuously touching me and talking and singing to me. I had been kissed by death, but refused to return the kiss.

I am sure that many other things happened during my time in the ICU, some of which I am not aware of to this day. Others, in my view, are unnecessary to share. Suffice it to say that I had a tremendous medical team, who possessed many varied skills and specialties to facilitate my recovery. Along with my loyal and dedicated family members and friends, they were clearly a blessing.

There are, however, some things that remain in my mind that I would like to mention. Although I was no longer comatose, I was heavily sedated and remained on a respirator, feeding tube, and other life-support systems. In order for me to get to the next level of recovery, my lungs had to relearn how to breathe on their own, which was enormously difficult.

In the midst of his worldwide travels as a senior project manager for Comverse Technologies, my brother called me many times every day. A nurse would put the phone to my ear, as I was trying to relearn how to breathe on my own, and Eric would say, "Gulp the air, brother. Try to swallow it." He would say in a slow, methodical, deep voice, "Just breathe slow and deep, one breath at a time."

Rabbi Dubrowski, who had become a friend of mine over the years, would come to my bedside and pray for me. While I was still comatose, he came to the ICU every Saturday night after sundown, and conducted the *Havdalah* service by my side.[138] My nephew Benny, my brother's oldest son, who studied on an intense track in a prominent yeshiva in Israel, mobilized his contacts to pray for me. Benny believes that the power of prayer is magnified by the scholarly level of the people who are praying.

My Uncle Harvey, who lived in Phoenix at the time, had his wife, my Aunt Toby, a talented pianist, record a cassette of her playing soothing music. My family members played it at my side while I was in a coma, although I never consciously heard it.

My children, my sister, Norman Linton, Neil Cantor, Richard Gorbaty, and my brother (when he was in Tampa, and by cell phone when he was not) would all come into my ICU room during the limited time they were allowed to visit during each hour. They would all talk to me, sing to me, or touch me, hoping that they would be able to get through to me on some level. They never gave up or stopped. One time, when I was heavily sedated and still connected to the respirator and other life-support and monitoring systems, they put a cell phone to my ear as they sang "Happy Birthday" to my son.

---

[138]The *Havdallah* is the service that is performed at the end of the Sabbath each week.

When I heard Andrew's voice, I unconsciously tried to get out of bed to go to him, but had to be held down. After that, they tied me to the bed.

There was another time, when I was not responding to my treatments, that Norman Linton said to me, "Sandy, if you recover from this next year for your birthday, I am going to buy you a brand new red Cannondale touring bike."

But I just lay there, totally unresponsive. Minutes later, as he was leaving, I lifted my legs and started moving them as if I were cycling. Apparently, that was quite a sight, but I have no memory of any of it.

When I finally regained full consciousness, I was challenged by having to learn how to breathe without a respirator and eat without a feeding tube. It might seem that those would be easy things to do, but they proved to be extremely challenging and required great effort. I was amazed, however, by the level of care, competency, and patience under demanding conditions that the professionals and staff of the ICU provided. They really helped me to overcome the hurdles I was facing as I adjusted to my newfound condition.

There was one nurse in particular who was amazing. She was highly involved in my care, and my family and friends later told me that she was involved with them as well throughout my ordeal. Apparently, she even cried with them at one point. No doubt, even in this medically restricted setting, she and I shared a mutual chemistry. Sometimes, people are simply drawn to each another and connect on multiple levels.

There are so many other stories about that medical crisis, most of which would probably bore anyone but me. I do, however, want to mention my New York Yankee tickets. Every year, I have season tickets for the Yankees' spring training in Tampa. My seats are incredible: on the first base line, right behind the Yankees' dugout. I always take clients or friends to the games, all-of whom really prize sitting in those wonderful seats. In 2000, spring training arrived while I was in the hospital. My sister and her boyfriend took care-of getting tickets to some of the people on my list of invitees. After I came out-of the coma, I gave tickets to some of the nurses and staff members who were helpful to me. They all loved the seats, and going to the games became the talk of the Cardiac Intensive Care Unit.

Recovering sufficiently for me to be transferred to a private room from the unit was a monumental step. Initially, I remained on a catheter, intravenous tubes, feeding tubes, and oxygen through the opening in my trachea, as well as through my nostrils. At that point, I didn't know that I had had a tracheotomy. I only knew that there were times when I couldn't breathe and was full-of something in my throat. Then the nurses would perform a procedure called "suctioning," which I didn't realize was extracting the accumulation of fluid

154

from my throat. I only knew it helped.

Slowly, ever so slowly, I began to rehabilitate. At first, my only means of communicating was by writing. I was still unable to talk because of the tube in my trachea. Nevertheless, I started to walk, tubes and all—initially, just from the bed to the door of the room and back. Then a little farther. And then a little farther still, until I could walk completely around the floor. Of course, in the beginning, I needed someone to assist me. However, with persistence and determination, I started to be able to do it myself, albeit with the support of a walker. Eventually, I didn't even need that.

The challenge was on, and I rose to it. I was intent on recovering. From one time around the perimeter of my wing, which was originally a big accomplishment, I got to the point over the next two weeks or so where I could go around twice, and then three times, and then four times. With each increase came new challenges, but I was determined to push the envelope to the limit. The trick was to learn what the limit was and not go beyond it. Taking baby steps was the key.

I vividly remember what a feeling of accomplishment it was the day my catheter was removed. I also remember the day I could stand by the sink and mirror and wash my hair and shave by myself.

As a dedicated exercise enthusiast before this major medical event, I found that walking was not the most difficult part of this phase of my recuperation. The most difficult part was learning how to breathe again. I remember thinking at the time that my compromised condition would never end and that I would have to live like this for the rest of my life. I was so scared of having to live in a diminished capacity. I knew that was the wrong way to think, but my emotions overtook my logic. Ultimately, I had to "trick my mind" into believing that I would transcend this situation and prevail.

As I started to recover and slowly regain strength, I became aware of another nurse who took a liking to me. We interacted the best we could without my being able to talk. She would come to my room during her breaks and read books to me. As she talked, I would do the best I could to respond by writing notes to her on a pad. Later, she would shave me and wash my hair. She was a very exotic and interesting woman. Although not especially attractive physically, she had an inner beauty and presence that transcended anything the physical lacked. But there was no question that we had an energy and a special friendship between us.

When my friend Jerry Faitelson made a special trip from Buffalo just to see me, I was delighted, although I couldn't talk to him. It was enough just to be together.

My cousin Renee Cooperman, who lived in Arizona, also made a special effort to see me as a representative of her family.

Many local friends, including Doug and Maureen Cohn, came by. Doug has always been a close friend and mentor to me—sort of an older brother figure. When my health insurance company wanted me to transfer to a less expensive rehabilitation facility, Doug and Maureen offered to have me stay at their home, rent a hospital bed, and have their housekeeper assist private duty nurses until I recovered enough to go home. Fortunately, I was able to remain in the hospital long enough until I was discharged to my own home.

I have been so blessed in my life with friends and other special people. Having been blessed with such special friends humbles me greatly.

Other friends wanted to come see me and help in any way they could, but they were discouraged from doing so by my sister and brother, who thought it was best for me to recover on my own. One such friend was Ken Kaufman, who was scheduled to fly to Italy with his new girlfriend (who is now his wife). He was prepared to cancel his trip to be there with me. When my family explained to him that there was nothing he could do to help, he went to Italy and got updates about my condition from my family by e-mail.

When the day finally came for me to be discharged, my sister and her boyfriend came to pick me up. I had made arrangements to have all of the flowers, balloons, cookie baskets, and other gifts for me sent over to the children's area of the hospital, insisting that they be given to disadvantaged children. Before I left the hospital, my attendants, at my request, wheeled me back to the Cardiac Intensive Care Unit where I had spent so much time, dependent on life-support systems and mostly in a comatose state. When we got there, I was shocked to see the room and the bed I had been in. The room was filled with the latest medical equipment, and the bed was so high-tech that it could actually chill me to lower my temperature. Seeing it all was intense.

The staff who were working on that shift were delighted to see me. Every one of them told me what a miracle it was that I was alive.

When I finally got outside for the first time in a month and a half, I was greeted by a beautiful sunny day with a bright blue sky and fresh, crisp air. My appreciation of life and the miracle of a new day was spectacular to me. The sight of a bird flying by was magnificent.

When I got home, I was somewhat disoriented by being away from the security of the hospital. Also, I was totally weak, fragile, and uncertain about my prognosis.

My family had arranged for me to be attended by a private duty nurse, Angie Medina, who was very comforting and helpful. I hurt all over, and couldn't even stand in the shower, but had to sit on a special seat while Angie bathed me.

My hands and fingers shook all the time like someone with Parkinson's disease, and I was cold all the time. I couldn't tolerate air conditioning, and had to be bundled under blankets and robes. Although the doctors wanted me to get out of bed and move around or change positions, I could only do so for very limited amounts of time, and spent most of the day and night napping.

That very first night home in my own bed was very difficult for me because I was frightened of the dark like a little child, even though I tried to act "grown up." Eventually, I overcame my fears and was able to sleep by inserting Andrea Bocelli's CD *Sogno* ("Dream") in a CD player by the side of my bed. Bocelli sings a duet on that album with Celine Dion entitled "The Prayer," which I loved, so I had the CD player set to repeat that song over and over again all night. The soothing music, the lyrics, and the voices filled the silence of the night, comforting me and eventually enabling me to sleep.

Rachael and Andrew flew down from Maryland to be with me two days after I got home. They brought a special pillow with them, which was designed to ergonomically support my neck and spine. Spending time with them in my own bedroom was the highlight of this period of recovery. I told them that hearing their voices when I was in a coma had comforted me when I was in that dark ethereal space. They didn't know that I had heard them, so this was a very emotional moment, and we "Three Mahrskateers" had tears in our eyes.

I came out of all this intent on recovering, pushing the envelope to the limit but not beyond. I did everything in my power to transcend the illness and disease. My role model for this approach was my dear friend Doug Cohn, who had a rare serious form of anemia, which just came upon him out of nowhere. As is his style in so many things, however, Doug chose to make the best of his life. As he would typically say about many things, "Just get on with it." He used to joke around by saying that he was the cover story on *Platelets Monthly Magazine*.

Up to that point in my medical odyssey, I never fully comprehended what had happened to me and what I was facing. All I knew was that I wanted to get back in shape again. My creed was recovery, and I focused all my energy on that. My muscles were atrophied from spending a month and a half in bed, and I was totally disoriented, overwhelmed by the list of restrictions and instructions from my various doctors. I was clear, though, that I would do everything in my power to get strong. As in medieval times, when a gauntlet was dropped to signify the start of a joust, I was committed to staying the course. But that proved to be one of the most difficult tasks I ever undertook in my life.

I clearly remember my first walk outside. I had to muster every ounce-of energy just to move along my driveway and through the little parking area in front of my house. I immediately realized that walking outside required much more effort than walking through the corridors of the hospital. But my doctors were very clear that the only exercise I could do was walk. So, walk I did. Twice a day, every day. Each day a little more. I remember thinking, *What a truly remarkable machine the human body is.*

When people asked to visit me or bring something over, I would ask them to walk with me instead. I couldn't walk alone, since I had to have a water bottle and my cell phone with me, and a companion just in case anything went wrong. My co-walkers included Angie Medina, Neil Cantor, Richard Gorbaty, Dickie Garrett, Murray Garrett, Bonnie Gorbaty, my sister Marilyn, Bill Suskauer, Steven and Kevin Cohen, and Dick Coley.

Ever so slowly, I started getting back into shape, walking a little farther each day. I kept saying to myself, "It's not what happens to me that matters, but how I *deal* with what happens to me."

One day, Angie drove me in her car to Sam's Club. I had to take a special foam pillow with me to protect my chest from the seatbelt, since the surgery had broken my ribs and cracked my chest bone. When I entered the store, I was immediately overwhelmed by its enormous size, although I had been there countless times before my illness. I tried to walk at first by holding on to the handle of a shopping cart for support, but I ended up having to use a handicapped motorized cart. That taught me what it is like for people who require that type of apparatus for even the simplest tasks.

When people asked how I was, I borrowed the line from my friend Doug Cohn, paraphrasing it for my own situation: "I'm the new cover story on *Aorta Monthly Magazine.*"

My sister and her boyfriend stayed with me until she was satisfied that I was on the road to recovery. By then, Passover was coming up, so Rachael and Andrew arrived for the Seders. I was still wearing my bathrobe all the time, since I was incredibly cold—literally, chilled to the bone. Everyone else in the house was warm, but I couldn't stand the slightest chill, which would be magnified many times over. Because my hands were still shaking, I couldn't hold a fork or a spoon without shaking and trembling.

At the first Seder, I had a small sip of wine, and was amazed that I felt a buzz from it.

"I'll make you a cup of coffee or tea to settle you down," my sister said.

"No," I said. "I like it."

When everyone left after Passover, Richard Gorbaty made a special trip to be with me, the next weekend. He went on walks with me and helped me to adjust to being alone.

During the months from Passover through the summer, I religiously pursued my exercise and rehab program. My close friend and client Barry Cohen, Esq., had two twin sons, Steven and Kevin. Steven, who throughout his life had undergone open-heart surgeries, nevertheless frequently came by to walk with me. His brother Kevin, who had my blood type, donated blood when I needed it while I was in the hospital, and when I was home, he came by to walk with me. All these people were amazingly supportive during those early months of recovery.

Since I was not allowed to do anything but walk, lifting weights was strictly off limits. As a result, my muscles atrophied even further. I was eventually able to work a little bicycling into my exercise regimen, but not much. As a matter of fact, my surgeons had told Norman Linton, with whom I had often cycled in the past, that I would *never* ride again the way I used to. Perhaps I would be able to ride around the neighborhood, but never again any great distances or at high speeds. I had to be totally aware of my heart rate, since my cardiologist didn't want it to go above 118 bpm, and he wanted my blood pressure to stay as low as possible.

It was especially hard for me not to be able to work out with weights. Over the years, I had learned to love my weight workouts and was proud of the physique I had developed. Now my sense of my physical fitness was at a low level. I felt out of shape and had not yet learned patience. I now realize that I had so much to be grateful for, but back then I was totally impatient with my recovery process, and started to feel a little sorry for myself. I now realize how ridiculous that was, and what a mistake I made. Those feelings would prove to lead me down an unnecessary detour from my road to recovery.

In business and in my personal finances, I was overwhelmed by having to use numbers. I simply couldn't perform certain basic cognitive and mathematical functions, which was totally frustrating to me. In some ways, I felt helpless. This incapacity was the byproduct of the particles of blood and other material lining the inside of my aorta, which broke away when my aorta was clamped while I was placed on the heart-lung bypass machine. Those particles apparently shot up to my brain, which is what had caused the ministroke in the first place. There could be no doubt that I was experiencing varying degrees of diminished capacity in some areas of my cerebral functioning

After the summer and heading into the fall, I fell into a funk, during which

I was depressed, despondent, and stayed home all the time, excluding myself from all social interaction. When I stopped walking on a regular basis, I gained weight and got into an even deeper slump. From starting my recovery process full steam ahead and focusing on whatever was necessary to get back, I was now totally ineffective, feeling sorry for my situation and the new limitations on my lifestyle. I now know how silly, sad, and unnecessary those feelings were.

Finally, out of desperation, I went to see Douglas Uzzell, Ph.D., a psychologist and friend, who helped me to reframe things to get back on track. Most of all, he reminded me of a technique I had written about years before, entitled "The Process," which appears in Chapter 17, above, and is repeated here:

THE PROCESS
(or how to deal with and respond to a stressful situation)

- Feel it. (What does it feel like under the emotion?)
- Honor the feeling.
- Find the fear or stressful feeling and face it.
- Do the first small task to start to relieve it. (Eat the elephant technique: How do you eat an elephant? One bite at a time.)
- Recognize the tendency to overreact, and defer it.
- Do not allow emotions to cause obsession.
- Seek to fully understand the issue.
- Know that there is a course of action and correction for everything.
- Use the Serenity Prayer as an affirmation. ("Grant me the serenity to accept the things I cannot change, the courage to accept the things I can, and the wisdom to know the difference.")
- Ask, "What difference will this make years from now?"
- Don't just react, be patient until the time is right, and then be proactive.
- Realize that no matter how bad the incident or situation may seem, "this too shall pass."
- Repeat all of the above as many times as necessary.

In December 2000, following a suggestion from Neil Cantor, I bought a treadmill, which I incorporated into my exercise regimen, and used it regularly as one of my main physical activities. That medical odyssey caused me to experience a full gamut of emotions, with many bumps along the way. I tried very hard to transcend all the highs and lows of my situation as I proceeded on a path of recovery. One of the most effective means of accomplishing that was by getting my body, mental state, and life in general back to where they should have been. It was one of the hardest challenges I have ever undertaken in my life.

As a result of all those experiences, literally every aspect of my life changed. I had to travel less frequently to see my children. I was unable to work with the same degree of effectiveness. I was unable to go out very often. My sleep patterns changed. I required medications on a daily basis. My doctors and I had to constantly monitor my condition. And the list goes on and on. To keep myself on a positive track, I constantly repeated the mantra: "My past does not equal my future."

I became determined that the up-and-down roller coaster ride of pain, the physical and emotional handicaps, and the ever-pervasive mode of being in and out of depression and loneliness would *not* be a part of my life. I built up to a point where I was able to return to the Harbour Island Athletic Club (HIAC). My friend Neil White, a personal trainer at HIAC, went around to the various machines with me with a blood pressure device to determine the amount of weight I could lift and what my corresponding blood pressure was for each exercise. The amounts of the weights were very small and seemingly insignificant; however, I was determined, and I did it. Baby steps initially. Only three days per week of resistance training. But after almost a year, I was back, and it felt great.

Norman Linton bought me the new Cannondale Road Bike that he had promised when I was in a coma, and I slowly began to ride it more and more as a supplement to my exercise and fitness routines. I made up my mind that I would be patient, gradually building up to being able to go greater distances. Patience and persistence were the keys.

Then I bought a dog, a purebred Weimaraner, which my children and I named "Hombre." I knew that he would be a lot of work, but I also knew that because of having him, I would be forced to be more active, getting out of the house and walking more. I would walk around the block at least twice a day for Hombre to perform his bodily functions, or I would take additional walks on Bayshore Boulevard, or I would go to the dog park to let him play with other dogs, while I interacted there with other dog owners.

Furthermore, although I had always been a voracious reader, I disciplined myself now to really tax my brain. First of all, I bought books on a variety-of topics, some very technical and detailed, and forced myself to read them and study them carefully. Subjects that I would never have normally chosen to read about, I forced myself to understand, one paragraph at a time. Then I started to write about this medical odyssey, which forced me to concentrate and was cathartic. I was determined to challenge and retrain my brain, forcing myself to work it as hard as I was working my body.

A mutual friend introduced me to a man in my neighborhood, Wayne, who had gone through a similar experience—although his was more recent, at a different hospital, and under slightly different conditions. When we met, Wayne and I bonded instantly. For a month or so, we walked together twice a week in the mornings, with Hombre accompanying me. Wayne and I talked about our ordeals and our individual approaches to recovery. He wasn't as committed as I was to a rigid exercise regimen. But observing him strengthened my resolve to recover. I was working hard at reinventing myself.

At some point, a new neighbor, Guy Joseph, who was a recently retired military officer, rented the townhouse next door to mine. We would go out with Hombre during what I refer to as my "warrior's creed" period, becoming better and better friends as we walked on Bayshore in the evenings. Guy supplemented my warrior's approach with e-mails that were on target and motivating. For example:

From: gjoseph
To: mahr
Wednesday, March 20, 2002, 9:48 AM

Morning, Sandy,

Here is a call to arms for a Warrior such as yourself. You're on track, and I can tell that you will let nothing stand in your way. "Forget past mistakes. Forget failures. Forget everything except what you're going to do now and do it." —William Durant, founder of General Motors
Happy hunting, my friend, have a great workout today!

Your friend,
Guy

From: gjoseph
To: mahr
Thursday, March 21, 2002, 9:57 AM

Morning, Sandy,

I just wanted to wish you a safe workout today—go get 'em, partner!
"Believe and act as if it were impossible to fail." —Kettering
I didn't have time to send you draft documents last night, but I plan on doing so this evening. Let me know if you're going to strut tonight.

Guy

From: gjoseph
To: mahr
Monday, March 25, 2002, 10:25 AM

Sandy,

Have a great workout—how was the bike ride this weekend? This is 8 or 9 straight days of working out? Hang in there, partner, you're doing great!!!
Here is something for you:
"Success is in our ability to learn from the past, adopt new ideas and actions in the present, and to challenge the future."
Let me know if you are going to walk this evening—I'm there if you are.

Guy

My friend Chuck Navarro, whom I had hired to work with me when I started my business in Buffalo many years ago, came to be with me during a particularly frustrating time in my recovery. When I first met him, he was over 65, retired, and a former manager of the Brunswick Company. I was 28 when I hired him to work for me as a manager in my fledgling company. As of this writing, I had known him for more than twenty-five years. In addition to our relationship at work, we always enjoyed a very special intellectual friendship, which revolved around philosophical discussions and a mutual passion for reading books. He moved from Lockport, New York, to the Daytona Beach area to live with his son. Chuck was 91 years old when I wrote this, but still active, vital, fit, and vigorous. Since then he has passed on. His being with me for a few weeks during my medical odyssey was comforting and reassuring.

The final step that enabled me to nail my recovery and get to the level that I am at now was "framed" for me by Neil Cantor. While we were talking one day, he helped me to come up with a program called "90 Days and Reassess." At that point, I knew that I was going to steel myself with "Iron Will," and had come up with the concept of doing so with my "Warrior's Creed." Neil told me that I needed to give myself 90 days and stay strictly on the program. In the past, I had learned how easy it is to get discouraged after trying to effect a major change in my life. When I didn't see the results I had hoped for, I would sometimes give up after thirty or sixty days.

Nevertheless, I liked Neil's idea, and started the Warrior's Creed: "This Is the Year This Warrior Will Conquer the Undisciplined Areas of His Life." I stuck to the program like glue, literally transforming myself to incredible levels. Although I prevailed, I learned that recovery is a painstaking process, the keys to which are persistence, patience, and intelligent decision-making.

A little more than two years after all this began, I wrote the following e-mail to some of my family members and close friends:

Subj: 16.58 miles nonstop…at about 15 miles per hour
Date: 5/5/2002 12:27:27 PM Eastern Daylight Time
From: mahr
Just sharing and letting you know that this morning was a milestone for me, something that I have not accomplished; however, have been looking forward to since my surgery. I biked 16.58 miles nonstop at approximately 15 mph. (Actually, as some of you will recall when I celebrated my 50th birthday by biking 50 miles, this is approximately the same route that I biked three times that day.) It is a big accomplishment for me, something I have been working on since the day I woke up from the coma and learned about what happened to me. It is by no means what I intend to accomplish; however, it is something the doctors and many others never expected me to be able to do. I want to let you all know because you are the

164

ones I love and am closest to. I want you to know that I continue to commit to being a warrior and a work in process; it has just taken me a little longer than I had expected.

The prognosis for my future is uncertain on a physiological level. I have a persistent flap in my aorta above the area of repair, extending into my aortic arch. It is not the type of situation that calls for prophylactic surgery, since that is high-risk and very complicated. My condition is being monitored regularly by my doctors with testing and annual CT Scans and Echocardiograms. Reports are then sent to the Baylor Medical Hospital in Houston, Texas. Dr. Joseph Cosselli is the leading medical expert on my condition, so if further surgery is required, it will probably be done there. However, I have chosen not to focus on the limitations or possibilities that may arise in the future. Rather, I have chosen to live my life in as full and as proactive a manner as possible. I am totally vested in the belief that I will continue to heal myself, making conscious decisions on a daily basis that will propel me along that path.

I do not fear death. I am fully aware that part of living is dying. The Theory of Dynamic Rejuvenation states that since we are either living or dying, there is no state of constancy. Each and every one of us eventually gets some medical condition; it is just a matter of what we get and when we get it. Some of us get things sooner, others later. What defines the quality of our lives is how we each choose to deal with whatever it is we get.

In September 2002, when I originally wrote this essay, I exercised on the treadmill every morning for at least 63 minutes. Additionally, at least five days per week, I usually did another 45 to 60 minutes of some sort of cardio, which was a combination of the elliptical machine, the rowing machine, and the recumbent bike at the Harbour Island Athletic Club. I did weight training at least three days per week. I generally went for a long bike ride once per week. I regularly walked and played with Hombre. My diet was and is mostly vegetarian—largely comprised of fresh raw fruits and vegetables, some fish, and various organic protein products.

As I continue to read and study, I have been finding that there are fewer subjects, especially those related to math, that frustrate me. I am learning many interesting new things that I normally would not have learned. My writing about all this has been cathartic, and hopefully people somewhere will benefit by being inspired by my example to overcome their own adversity and stay on the path of their recovery.

I prevailed, and so my earthly journey continues.

BACK IN THE DAY

An Interview of Sanford Mahr by Rachael Mahr[139]

(October 5, 2001)

(I am sitting down across from a man I've known all of my life. I am excited and curious about the new things I will soon discover about the person whom I most relate to in this world. He looks at me and gives me a warm smile; if I were nervous at all before, the nervousness has now passed and is replaced by intense curiosity and a need to know. I look right at my father and ask him about his experiences as a musician and as a producer of concerts and various rock 'n' roll bands in the late 1960s and early 1970s.)

SANFORD: I guess I was always a musician. I started loving music ever since I can remember. Actually, my mother and her family always told me stories about how I came by music naturally. Professional music in various forms has been in my family genes for generations. They traced it back to Russia in the early 1800s, when my great-great-grandfather toured the countryside as a cantor.

When I was in high school, I was in a popular band called The Counterpoints. In addition to playing the saxophone, I was in charge of getting all of the bookings for the band and taking care of all the business details. As

---

[139]Now married and Rachael Sarah Pollack

a matter of fact, as the years went on, I was part of a number of different bands. But no matter what band I was in, I always took care of the business arrangements. In later years, it became apparent to me that the "safe money" was to be made in the business part of the music, not in taking a chance at being a successful musician. In the late 1960s, my college years, I was a member of a band originally called *Bloor Street West*, which later transformed into a jazz fusion band called *The Gate To*. We played some of the finest jazz clubs in Buffalo, New York—among them, David's Table (later renamed St. George's Table), Gabriel's Gate, Jack's Cellar, The Cloister, and other select venues. We developed a following, and once, while we were playing at St. George's Table, the news crew that was covering a Buffalo Bills game came by, were taken by us, and asked if they could film us for the late news show. As luck would have it, a representative of The Playboy Clubs was in town to open a Playboy Club in Buffalo, and happened to see us on the news. That led to an association for a while gigging at various of their venues, not as a featured band, but as one of their lounge bands.

When I was living in Buffalo in the late 1960s and early 1970s, I attended many concerts, including some produced by the student body at the University of Buffalo. In those days, universities produced concerts. The group that coordinated those events at The State University of New York at Buffalo was called the UUAB. Basically, it was a group of students who put on concerts, and I became friendly with a couple of guys who were part of it. They understood the mechanics of putting on concerts, but lacked the business savvy to finance, market, and otherwise produce concerts on their own. So, I formed an association with them, utilizing their skills in running concerts, while I took care of all the other details. Soon, I started a company called Production Concepts, which initially I associated with UUAB, thereby giving me an entree into the otherwise closed circle of artists and their agents.

The next step was to book the bands. After a lot of research, I began contacting booking agencies in New York and Los Angeles. At first, I was met with many refusals, but finally I was able to book a concert featuring three R&B bands: Mandrill; Eddie Kendricks; and Funkadelic. The concert was held at Buffalo Memorial Auditorium. It took a lot of work to coordinate, but ultimately the concert was successful, and I was now on my way. The agencies wanted to see how well I could produce a concert, and after the success of my first concert, they started letting me take on bigger names.

As the producer of the concerts, I was in complete charge of every business aspect of the events, including advertising, security, ticket sales, seating, backstage arrangements, staging, catering, and hospitality suites for the artists.

My responsibilities included all the major and minor details pertaining to the events. I learned firsthand the true meaning of the saying, "The devil is in the details"—which I converted to "Excellence is in the details." My various responsibilities included: location of the performance, promotion, poster design and distribution, hiring of lighting and sound companies, marketing, radio and TV promotions, and arranging for the many requirements of the artists. I was in charge of every detail pertaining to putting on the show.

It was rewarding to me to be a part of what was happening in the music industry. I loved being a part of the music scene so much. Music and production as a whole had been such a major part of my life during the late 1960s and early 1970s. There were many advantages beyond the opportunity to make a lot of money, but there were some challenges, too. At times, it was really difficult to deal with some of the artists' attitudes and demands. It was great, though, to be able to meet so many different talented people. I met musicians, agents, managers, business people, record company executives, road crews, technicians, and TV and radio personalities.

My favorite band to produce concerts for was Orleans. At the time, I really liked their style and their music. They represented a holdover sound from the Woodstock era, but mixed it with the ever-evolving rock 'n' roll sound. They were very cool, yet regular people to hang around with.

ZZ Top, on the other hand, were more famous and more in demand at that time. They were a talented, successful, hard rock Texan band, but they definitely had an attitude that they were big stars and as such required special treatment.

Richie Havens, whose fame started at Woodstock, was perhaps one of the easiest musicians to work with.

But my favorite band of all time to work with on many levels was The Road, whose members, while I was a part of them, included in various iterations Nick DiStefano, Harry Stinson, Arnold Laux, Joe Hesse, Phil Hudson, Jerry Hudson, Jim Catino, and Ken Kaufman. The Road was a regional pop rock 'n' roll band, somewhat in the mold of the Beatles. I'm still very close with most of those guys. Our history runs deep, and we have shared some major times together—not just individual concerts, but tons of miles traveled on many road trips, many tours, and many recording sessions.

I am not sure that I would advise anyone to get involved in concert production at this time, unless it is as a part of a larger venue, such as special or online formats. As the saying goes, "Opportunity is a moving target, which changes with the times." As I always tell you and your brother, in order to be successful at anything, you need to position yourself with or in front of the trends. That way, you ride the waves. The media have changed dramatically since the 1960s and 1970s. Back then, there was no MTV or VH1. Nor were there MP3's or online music downloading, as is popular today. In the 1960s and 1970s, the only way people got to see their favorite musicians and bands was at live concerts or on TV. They could listen to the bands on the radio or on records. Although concerts are still being produced today, and some people find it to be a viable business, in my opinion it is not as readily accessible as it once was to newcomers. Therefore, if you lack previous experience with producing concerts, it is extremely difficult to get started in this day and age.

If I had a chance to go back and do it all again, I would probably do more producing of established acts. I would probably even associate myself in the early stages with an established production company before going out on my own to learn the ins and outs. I would then start producing concerts on my own. I would continue to expand my market area as I had started to by working with up-and-coming artists in smaller venues. Such artists I had begun to produce concerts for included Billy Joel and Linda Ronstadt, neither of whom were yet established artists. Nevertheless, I had a lot of fun back then. I learned a lot, met many interesting people, and made a fair amount of money.

BIRTHDAY LETTER TO MY FAMILY

S o…. Thank you ALL for being part of my life, and as such just your being in it is a MAJOR celebratory event for me. The high honor and privilege of sharing part of life's journey with you is truly magical.

> *Magic is as Magic was,*
> *and shall for ever be*
> *Those experiential moments shared*
> *with you*
> *My Family*
> *Throughout eternity.*

I believe a life is counted in ways more than can be quantified by numbers, more than by a marking of years passed, even more than by a marking of years to come.

As most of you know, I have always chosen to celebrate the day of one's birth rather than mourn the passing of one's death. My reasons are many, not the least of which is that the days of people's births start their earthly walk, giving them a beginning to lend their influence, creativity, and actions, if you will, to "people, places, and things"—thus performing "Tikkun Olam." *Tikkun* in Hebrew means "correction," and *Olam* means "Universe." So, in essence, the concept of Tikkun Olam is that each life has a purpose beyond mere existence to assist in perfecting the ongoing process of creation.

We are all a part of it. What we do each day by random yet intentional acts of kindness to people, places, and things we encounter are the essence of a life lived.

So, once again, among the gifts I am giving you this year in celebration-of the twentieth anniversary of my fiftieth birthday is the concept of the Tree.

The concept of the Tree is something that I became aware of with great significance after my brother was married. After that, I asked my Uncle Harvey (my mother's brother) if he would take a couple of days off to show me the place where he and my mother were born and raised. Since both my parents were deceased, I wanted to learn firsthand about my roots. My uncle agreed, so we drove to a little town in the southern tier of New York State in the Allegheny River Valley, near the Pennsylvania border.

The town of Olean was small, and my uncle's and mother's childhood home was nestled near the banks of the Allegheny River. As we approached the house, we stopped at the top of a hill for a red light. As I looked down, the area was strikingly barren. The houses were small, and in their day perhaps lower-middle-class, but now they were clearly upper-lower-class at best. The neighborhood was barren, but from the top of the hill I could not help having my eyes drawn to a lone tree near the bottom.

When we drove to the house, we stopped directly in front of that tree. When I asked my uncle about it, he said that my mother planted it with my grandfather when she was a little girl. Wow! I thought that tree was clearly the only thing of beauty in the whole area, which was thanks to my beloved mother. Here is a picture of that tree, which I took that day

Figure 20: My Mother's Tree

171

I have tried over the years, and whenever possible with Rachael and Andrew, to agree that, wherever we live, we will plant a tree, and so far we have done that at each of our homes. I hope my children will continue that tradition and teach it to the generations that follow. By the way, the value-of the tree is much more than aesthetic, for each tree gives back to the Earth and its inhabitants and is life anew.

So…, in addition to my gifts to you for my birthday, a tree has been planted in Israel in your name and honor. The certificate in each of your names will be mailed to you directly.

(6th Day of March, 2019)

THIS VISUAL I CREATED SITS PROMINENTLY ON MY DESK, AND I REFER TO IT DAILY THROUGHOUT THE DAY

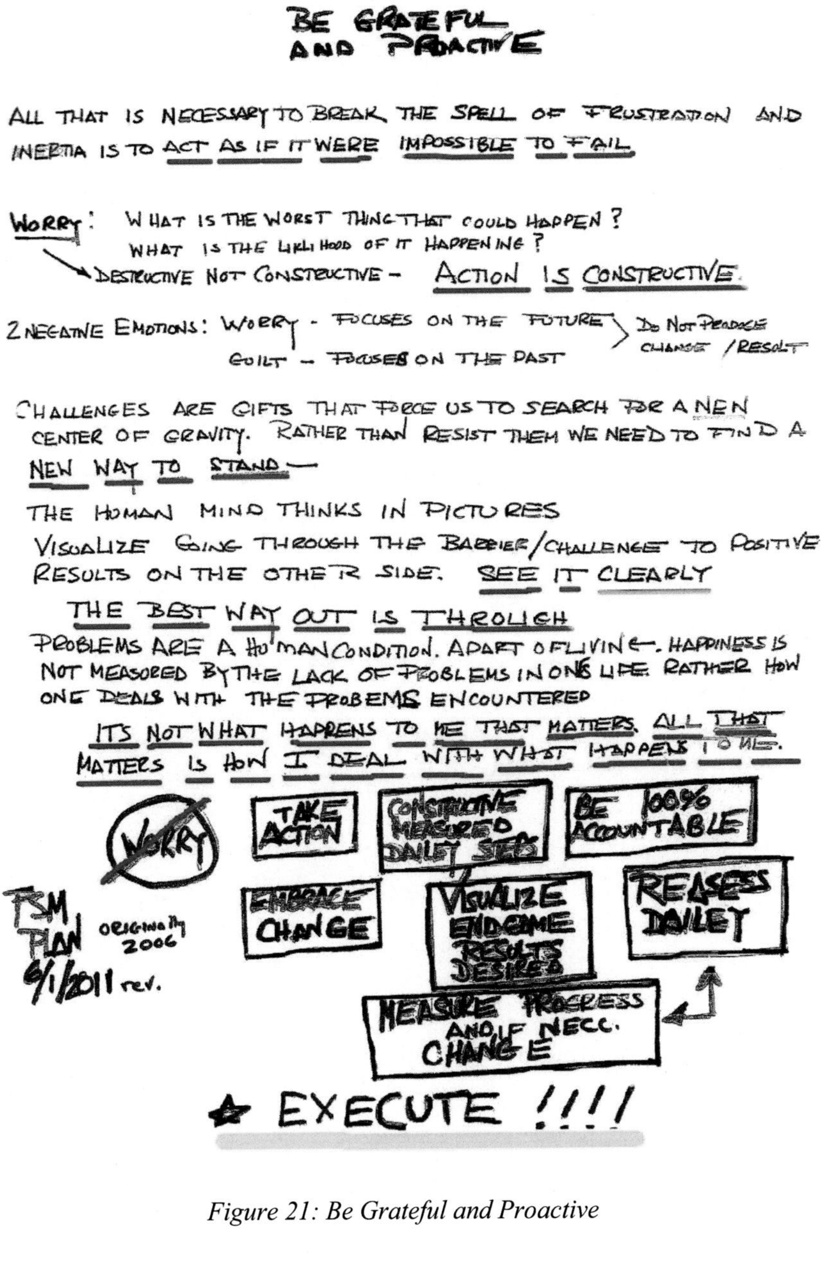

BE GRATEFUL
AND PROACTIVE

ALL THAT IS NECESSARY TO BREAK THE SPELL OF FRUSTRATION AND INERTIA IS TO ACT AS IF IT WERE IMPOSSIBLE TO FAIL

WORRY: WHAT IS THE WORST THING THAT COULD HAPPEN?
WHAT IS THE LIKLIHOOD OF IT HAPPENING?
DESTRUCTIVE NOT CONSTRUCTIVE - ACTION IS CONSTRUCTIVE

2 NEGATIVE EMOTIONS: WORRY - FOCUSES ON THE FUTURE
GUILT - FOCUSES ON THE PAST
DO NOT PRODUCE CHANGE / RESULT

CHALLENGES ARE GIFTS THAT FORCE US TO SEARCH FOR A NEW CENTER OF GRAVITY. RATHER THAN RESIST THEM WE NEED TO FIND A NEW WAY TO STAND —

THE HUMAN MIND THINKS IN PICTURES
VISUALIZE GOING THROUGH THE BARRIER/CHALLENGE TO POSITIVE RESULTS ON THE OTHER SIDE. SEE IT CLEARLY

THE BEST WAY OUT IS THROUGH
PROBLEMS ARE A HUMAN CONDITION. APART OF LIVING. HAPPINESS IS NOT MEASURED BY THE LACK OF PROBLEMS IN ONE'S LIFE. RATHER HOW ONE DEALS WITH THE PROBLEMS ENCOUNTERED

ITS NOT WHAT HAPPENS TO ME THAT MATTERS. ALL THAT MATTERS IS HOW I DEAL WITH WHAT HAPPENS TO ME.

WORRY

TAKE ACTION | CONSTRUCTIVE MEASURED DAILEY STEPS | BE 100% ACCOUNTABLE

EMBRACE CHANGE | VISUALIZE ENDGAME RESULTS DESIRED | REASESS DAILEY

RSM PLAN ORIGINALLY 2006 9/1/2011 rev.

MEASURE PROGRESS AND IF NECC. CHANGE

★ EXECUTE !!!!

Figure 21: Be Grateful and Proactive

173

BRUSHSTROKES ON THE LANDSCAPE OF LIFE

Written in the Judean Desert, Israel — 3 August 1999

Spoken at the Bell Caves, Israel, to the participants of the UJA Summer

Family III Mission

By F. Sanford Mahr

I am memorializing these personal thoughts and experiences at the prompting of Rabbi Michael Matusen, who happened to witness various conversations I had with my children, Rachael and Andrew, throughout the UJA Summer Family III Mission these past days.

Perhaps, then, the most succinct metaphor I am able to conjure up to summarize the experience I had by being in our homeland with my children and all of you is "brushstrokes on the landscape of life."

This week was a blessing to me for many, many reasons, not the least-of which was the opportunity to forge new friendships and enduring relationships in concert with the rediscovery of this portion of the planet we all inhabit. This sacred land we have been traveling and exploring resonates with the contributions of countless generations of an ancestral presence that each one of us here today shares in common. Yet, being here in these moments, these nows, these brief instances in the spectrum of time, and then to share them through the eyes of my children, has created a new reality and meaning for me.

This time.

On this mission.

In this approximately fiftieth year of Israel's recreation.

There have been so many sunsets and so many amazing sunrises.

As the sun sets and kisses the horizon,
while its touch gently lingers on the sky at dusk,
the promise of tomorrow and new beginnings permeates....

We witnessed the promise of a renewed Israel, the home of our people, the home of our lineage, the place that is now a homeland for all of us, my children as well as yours, and our grandchildren who are yet to be, and beyond.

This time, after many previous trips to Israel, I saw a land unfold before me in a new way—a land that has evolved over thousands of years, albeit on a circuitous path for our people. Nevertheless, and notwithstanding a lack of continuity, the impact of who we are and what we have sacrificed and created in this land was apparent to me, no matter where our tour guides led us.

It occurred to me that our life spans are limited in relation to the life span of this land—a land where the infinite has chosen to touch, bless, and breathe a magical formula of ultimate coexistence. Each of us has been given a paintbrush to add color to its landscape. We each have been gifted with a partnership in the creation process, which is and always will be ongoing and never-ending. We have all borne witness to the contributions that every generation before us made to this land—a land, I am sure you will agree, of amazement, wonder, and splendor. Each day we have been together has offered us glimpses of what this land has meant throughout all of history.

I felt the presence of those who contributed before us, and saw with you some of their contributions in every step we have taken during these past days. From the barren deserts of Abraham's time to the lushness of the Galilee, a painting unfolded before me—one with colors and layers of color applied by our ancestors. Each generation in its own way, according to the means, tools, knowledge, and technology available to it, added a few more brushstrokes to this ongoing masterpiece.

Yesterday, as I stood outside the re-creation of Abraham's tent, I looked out at the endless miles of sand and saw a vast canvas: the Judean Desert. It struck me that these sand dunes, these mountains and valleys, barren, uninhabited, desolate, and stark, must have been the Israel that Abraham encountered. It was complete with its inherent challenges, yet sprinkled throughout with the possibilities of a masterpiece waiting to be painted. Abraham painted the first few brushstrokes on the canvas before him. He started a picture with a base that cried out for continual coloring, and he added some color from his palate. Each subsequent generation with its own paintbrushes and palates contributed a few more brushstrokes, and the picture of the landscape of life that was Israel then and now appeared.

During these past days, all of us experienced the results of their efforts in all of their glory. The wonder of it all was greater than viewing the beauty of all the masterpieces hanging in museums and galleries throughout the world. Yet, the highs and lows of Israel's history, and the wear and tear of the Diaspora and conquering peoples, remain apparent and visible—perhaps, in simpler metaphoric terms, like some of the great works of Renaissance art, or the Egyptian pyramids for that matter, that have deteriorated and now require restoration by our generation.

When I looked over at our children, who were seated inside Abraham's tent in "Bible Land," they were watching the actors preparing bread, and the thought occurred to me that, through this trip, we have planted seeds in them. We have provided them with better points of reference of their history, people, and magical land. Soon, the paintbrushes will be passed to them and will be theirs to use. It will be our children who paint the next brushstrokes on the canvas of Israel. This week, we have given our children a palate of vast colors to take with them as they continue on their life journeys and grow into all that they can become. I hope the memories of their homeland will burn in their hearts and minds, allowing them to paint with a passion and zeal that will enable their children to look on with amazement, awe, and reverence at a landscape of life that exists nowhere else on this planet.

Yet, what of *us?* What else can *we* do? We must give of our resources to the best of our abilities. The commitment we maintain to giving can be likened to flowers planted on this landscape of life. The seeds have been sown that were our fathers' and grandfathers' contributions to the future flowers that will need to be planted. The brushstrokes now must come from our hands, to keep the palate of the landscape alive, vital, and full of color. Yet, what-of the future flowers that will need to be planted?

We must teach the next generation by example. We must replenish. We must always plant the seeds for new flowers, for it will be our children, grandchildren, great-grandchildren, their children, and their children who will watch them bloom with pride, joy, and happiness, serving as an example for them to do the same for those to come.

With that in my mind and heart, I can do no less than increase my humble financial contribution to UJA, and I pledge to increase it each and every year thereafter. I ask you all to consider doing the same.

> *Magic is as Magic was*
> *and will forever be*
> *That first moment when I met you, my Israel,*
> *throughout eternity.*

EULOGY FOR MY BROTHER, ERIC ARYEH M. MAHR

6 February 2010

(Delivered for me by Abraham Israel, founder of Hazon Yeshaya)

I am here as the personal emissary of Sanford Mahr, brother of Eric Mahr, "Aryeh Elter Mordechai Ben Shaya," to convey his words, since he has been restricted by physicians and family, based on his medical condition, not to make the long journey to Israel.

These, then, are the words he would have spoken himself:

What is the measure of one's life?

How does one recognize the depth of one's footprints left on the landscape of one's earthly existence?

A person's walk, although it begins with just a single step, followed by another and then another, eventually results in a journey through life. Whether the individual blazes new trails or follows paths previously taken by others is not important. Rather, what are of tantamount importance are the depth and markings that are left in the process. For some people, there are barely a grain or two of sand that have been shifted or displaced, let alone footprints. For others, the footprints are so deep that even the winds of time cannot erase them. They are indelibly marked to be followed and observed.

May I proffer that, in my view, the measures of a life lived (the footprints left or lack thereof) are evidenced by the kindness and acts one offers as he or she walks along the journey of life. Those acts of kindness have a side effect of defining the depth and breadth of one's footprints.

If a footprint were to be likened to an accomplishment, then the accomplishment must not be measured by material gain, artistic endeavor, or scientific discovery. Rather, the only measure is the random and continual actions of kindness and giving of oneself *or* the deployment of one's accumulated assets, creations, or inventions for the betterment of all humanity and all living things. The outline of the footprints, then, and their depth and breadth, are defined as above.

Eric Mahr "Aryeh ben Shaya," my brother, was a man whose very

177

existence touched and left footprints on a multitude of people, places, and things in all walks of life. For every day of his life, since he was a little boy, he performed random acts of kindness and always gave of himself to everyone he met along the way. Always.

He did that without effort. Without intent. Rather, his acts of kindness were a part of his very being, his very composition. They came to him as naturally as breathing air. My brother was a kind, loving, sweet soul from the day he was born to the moment I shared his very last breath with him.

As he took one step at a time and moved from one encounter to another, he left footprints. Nay, he blazed deep marks in the hearts and souls-of virtually everyone he encountered. In all my years with him as his older brother, I cannot recall one single human being who did not benefit from knowing and interacting with this gentlest of beings.

As a little boy walking home from grammar school in Buffalo, New York, he was hit by a car while crossing the street. The car didn't stop, nor did any passersby. Little "Ricky," as he was known then, was unable to walk or stand because his leg was broken. Yet, he dragged himself the two blocks home. When he got there, he matter-of-factly told our mother that he "might need a little help because I hurt myself." Not "Someone hurt me, Mommy." Not "I was hit by a car, Mom." Rather, "I might need a little help because I hurt myself." Even at that young and tender age, he did not blame. Somehow he took action, made it home, and got the help he needed.

As a young child, he started to exhibit his brilliance and intellectual prowess by memorizing the name of every single dinosaur. When each was displayed somewhere, he could literally name every one of them. In later years, he took to reading whole pages of the encyclopedia and just devoured information. He was a voracious reader. However, the world of comic books entered his life at an early age, and he became fascinated by them, and then by science fiction, of which he later became a huge collector.

Of course, this later was the baseline of some of the books he authored. I remember all too well when young Ricky, who was somewhat shy in his early years, stunned us all one day when he appeared in the living room of our home in blackface and pantomimed to Al Jolson songs. That was the end-of his youthful introversion and the beginning of his blossoming into the man loved by so many.

Although not a consummate athlete, he decided in high school that he wanted to play football, and with sheer will and determination he transformed himself to make the team, à la the character in the movie *Rudy*.

My brother followed in our father's footsteps by obtaining his Eagle Scout rank in the Boy Scouts—an undertaking that is accomplished by only a select few. Many begin; few complete.

Although I was more of an athlete, it was my brother who taught me how to run. After reading Jim Fixx's book on running, he trained himself to run at a 440 yard track. He always did that late at night, and one night he took me to the track and ran far more laps than I could, which amazed me. But he taught me how he trained, and made a long-distance runner out of me.

In his adult life, as many of you know, he wrote many books, all of them published by a company he created called Mahrwood Press. I believe that it was his fascination with comic books in his formative years and beyond that provided him with the creativity to author and publish books illustrated by famous graphic artists, which depicted events of the religious beliefs and history that he loved, in a manner not ever done before.

His life, his accomplishments, and his profound love of family were certainly modeled after the special relationship he had with our father. Yet, I believe that the course of his adult life was most deeply defined when, at the age of 18, he had to identify the body of our father, who was lying in a pool of blood after being savagely murdered by two young thieves who held up his pharmacy. Three years later, our mother died in his arms while he was trying to give her mouth-to-mouth resuscitation after she choked on a cookie, which induced cardiac arrest.

My brother then turned more fervently to Judaism for spiritual comfort. As a young boy, he had been trained in the Hebrew school of the Saranac Synagogue, and attended Judaic summer camps in central New York State during some summers. He took to his religious studies and practices with the same fervor and passion as he had earlier taken to dinosaurs, encyclopedias, football, and running. However, his turning to Judaism for spiritual comfort was modeled by our mother, when she insisted that he and I accompany her after our father's murder to twice daily minyans at the temple. It was there that Eric mastered dovening and chanting the prayers.

After our mother's death, as he pursued Judaism, he met his wife, Jody, and together they embraced Judaism with love, passion, and zeal as they raised their children. Their home was always filled with friends and family. No one was ever turned away. Everyone was welcome, and magically there was always more than enough for all of them.

I could go on and on, filling up hours of this day with stories of Eric Mahr. I could tell you about his successes and failures. He always used both of those to learn. Instead, I would encourage you to mention his name anywhere, and you will likely find someone who knew him or knew of him.

Hear me, people, wherever you may be. You have borne witness to the footsteps of a special being, a man so replete with kindness and giving in every step of his daily walk that, no matter where, no matter what the circumstances of your interaction with him, you felt his touch. You experienced his pure and unselfish giving. You realized his genuineness and caring.

I asked earlier, what is the measure of a man? My answer is to give you one yardstick that you can measure by…, and that is my brother, Eric Mahr.

Please allow me to share with you the last few hours of his life as I observed them. He flew under duress and stress to be at his father-in-law's funeral. His wife had flown ahead, since she was flying home to the United States from Israel to visit her father, and while she was in the air her father died. My brother delivered an eloquent eulogy for his father-in-law and carried with him words from his sons and a poem from his daughter that he also read. Within hours of the funeral and *shiva*, he attended with the *Chevra Chadisha* to our uncle's body, who unbelievably had also died, and the funeral was to be the next day. My brother communicated with me via text message how difficult and intense it was for him, since he was so close to our uncle, as were we all.

On the morning of our uncle's funeral, twenty-four hours after his father-in-law's funeral, Eric handled pressing personal business matters by phone, e-mail, and text. He then met with our sister and me, since it was the first time that all three of us were together in many years. Then, before we all left to go together to our uncle's funeral, so he could deliver yet another eulogy, he stopped before walking out the door, went back inside, and said he would be back in a few minutes, since he hadn't yet put on his *tfellin*. When he returned, we all left for the funeral, where my brother fulfilled a promise to our uncle, made many years before, that he would be with him the next time he was in Buffalo. Then he started his eulogy.

In mid-sentence, he suddenly collapsed, and despite every effort by me, and later by the paramedics, to resuscitate him, he left this Earth.

The sun has perhaps set on my brother's physical journey, but not his mark on ours….
Rest in peace, my brother, you did not die in vain
Rest in peace, my brother, the world will miss you so
Rest in peace, my brother, we will always keep your memory alive
Rest in peace, my brother, we will live our lives with you forever in our hearts

Rest in peace now, brother, you will not be forgotten, and the rich legacy you have left, your teachings and acts of kindness, will live on and on and on

My dear sweet, oh so special brother, rest in peace.

BIRTHDAY MESSAGE TO MY BROTHER, ERIC ARYEH MAHR,

TEN YEARS LATER

8.November.2020 — HAPPY BIRTHDAY, BRO — Today would have been the birthday of my late brother, Eric Aryeh Mahr z'l. It's been ten years since his passing. Although I remember him daily throughout the year, I choose to celebrate the day he began his life journey by recalling the many contributions he made, as well as the many memories he left for those who knew and loved him, rather than mourn the day he passed. It is, after all, not that he died that matters, but rather that he lived.

My dearest brother,
I have visited the hill where spirit dwells.
I have visited with you.
I have visited in solitude.
I have journeyed from it with you and now alone.
Your spirit dwells not on it where you once were its king,
but rather in the valleys, rivers, and trails where your presence still sings.
A saluté, my brother, for life lived, love given, lessons taught,
and for the exemplary manner you showed all.
You live on in the hearts, minds, and souls of those of us
who have been touched by your being during this
iteration of physical being.
These words burn indelibly into the journal of life.
Happy Birthday, Bro!

25 November 2015, Thanksgiving Day

"THANKSGIVING NOT A DAY. THANKSGIVING A WAY."

Thanksgiving is not a day, it's a way.
Today the way is to be thankful for not having everything we desire,
rather to look towards achieving and forward to the possibilities there are to come.

Today the way is to be thankful for not necessarily knowing,
rather for the opportunity to *learn*.

Today the way is to be thankful for adversity
and the *growth* that comes from transcending its difficulty.

Today the way is to be thankful for limitations,
they provide opportunities to *improve*.

Today the way is to be thankful for each new challenge living presents,
within each lies opportunity for further developing *strength* and *character*.

Today the way is to be thankful for mistakes…
recognition/acknowledgement…, therein lie *teachings*.

Today the way is to be thankful for being tired and weary
from concentrated effort and persistence,
it is an indicator of the difference we are on the path of making.

Although it may seem easiest to be thankful for what is perceived as good,
the life of richness and fulfillment comes
by being thankful for what is less than good.

Gratitude. A force whose power turns negatives into positives.
The discovery of ways to be appreciative of troubles/challenges
transforms them into blessings.

Thanksgiving Day signifies a point in time when we *come together,*
reminded to give thanks.
We need not nor should not wait
until that next "timepoint" to come together or be reminded.
Thanksgiving is not a day, it's a way.

> We can make every day one of thanksgiving;
> we can acknowledge each day as robed as a unique gift.
> So then, give a hug for no reason;
> So then, say, "I love you," *just because;*
> So then, share a smile with a stranger;
> So then, perform a random yet intentional act of *kindness*
> to people, places, and things
> you meet along the way…, each day;
> So then, count blessings.
> So then, appreciate everything and everyone.
> So then, end each day with no regrets.
> So then, start each day full of expects.
> Sing loudly and clearly to each other:
> "Thank you, my dear, dearest of friends and family,
> for sharing, caring, laughing, and crying with me.
> We are truly blessed to have each other,
> and together to be a part of this greater whole called life."
> *Thanksgiving is not a day, it's a way.*

TO BE A WARRIOR

To be a warrior means that the margin for error is reduced to an infinitesimal degree.

—F. Sanford Mahr

Life is a series of natural and spontaneous changes. Don't resist them: that only creates sorrow. Let reality be reality. Let things flow naturally forward in whatever way they like.

—Lao Tzu[140]

I was at a point in my life and along the path of my recovery journey where I was ready to take my proactive ways to a new level to prevail over certain areas of my life that had previously been elusive. I chose the image of becoming a warrior to transcend what may have been holding me back from what I wanted to achieve. On a bike ride to Tarpon Springs, Florida, with my friend Neil Cantor, during our conversation he synergistically helped me to develop the following creed: "This is the year this warrior will conquer the remaining undisciplined areas of his life."

Being a warrior has always fascinated me—not a warrior who focuses on battle and victory at the expense of others, but rather a warrior who engages proactively in activities that will produce long-lasting, positive, and meaningful results.

---

[140]Available at https://en.wikipedia.org/wiki/Laozi/.

Warriors share traits
A Warrior's journey continues
Toward new goals, undeterred,
Head-on,
Straight, like an arrow shot from a bow
Through the obstacles of new challenges,
Past the limitations of negativity,
Transcending the mediocrity of the majority,
While ever maintaining the respect of many who admire his
Joie de vive....
A Warrior's journey continues...,
Undaunted by distractions,
Undeterred in his resolve,
Committed to doing only what is right,
Leading by exemplary action,
On a course of predetermined achievement...,
Accomplishment after accomplishment...,
Success after success.
There are those who rise with him
Up to the levels of expectation he places upon them.
There are those left along the way,
Unable to sustain their focus through the trials and tribulations
a Warrior's journey entails.
But He, He is a Warrior....
Make no mistake about it,
An instinctive predator of weakness and lack of accomplishment....
A Warrior whose main weapon is his honed "Iron Will."
His journey is fast-paced, persistent, and filled with action.
Nevertheless, he always lends a helping hand, offering guidance
to those in need along his way.
A Warrior's journey continues...
The Purpose: Evolution
The Arena: Daily Life
The Time: Now
The Method: Simple Action
The Process: Execution
The Creed: This Warrior will conquer the remaining undisciplined areas
of his life

ONE WARRIOR'S MUSINGS

Say not in grief, "He is no more," but live in thankfulness that he was.

—Hebrew Proverb

Neil J. Cantor 1 (NJC) was a fiercely loyal, extremely close friend and mentor to me. He was an exemplary warrior. He was committed to making the world a better place, always striving to "do the right thing," and helping others to grow and become the best they could be. With his wife, Diane, by his side, he became invincible. He was one half of "DiaNeil." As a whole, they were Camelot. Diane's unexpected death a few years before Neil's created a void that was never filled, despite his "Iron Will," his character, and his persona. After eighty-six years of his Earthly walk, he simply closed his eyes one morning at breakfast and didn't open them again. It was almost as if he were finished with life.

NJC told me for years that he disciplined himself every day to concentrate on and say an affirmation. During his later years, although Neil was not religiously observant, he was reverent. Somewhere along the way, he added to his daily affirmation the first line of the ancient Hebrew prayer, "The Shema."

After Diane died tragically in 2010, Neil and I continued, of course, to talk many times. We never missed a day during that period to include the recitation together of his affirmation, which was as follows:

Thy will be done this day.
Today is a day of completion.
I give thanks for this perfect day.
Miracle shall follow miracle,
and wonders shall never cease.
Sh'ma Yis'ra'eil Adonai Eloheinu Adonai Echad.
Hear O Israel, the Lord is our God, the Lord is One.

187

Over the many years, Neil and I talked about and worked on many things together during our daily interactions, including but not limited to our many long walks, bike rides, dinners, lunches, telephone calls, etc. The following are some of the things he and I thought of for me to one day share as part-of his legacy. Some are in the first person because he told them to me while I was writing. Others are from my notes and observations of him:

I do not nor will not suffer fools gladly.

Sandy, for people like us, self-starters highly motivated and hard-driving, work expands or contracts with the amount of time you allocate to it.

We all have the same twenty-four hours in a day. How we each choose to use them is what separates us.

NJC has what I labeled "Iron Will" (see Chapter 17)—total discipline, which he maintained through extreme constant and never-ending self-talk.

Be prepared, Sandy. I am always prepared for the worst. That way, if it comes, I know how to deal with it.

You must develop a process to deal with adversity. No matter how hard it is, you must persist.

If you fully believe in what you want one percent more than one hundred percent, you will get it. There must not be any doubt in your mind.

NJC always created an environment of high expectations of the people around him. They would either rise to that level or fall out of his life.

The will to win is not nearly as important as the will to prepare to win.

The definition of luck is adequate preparation meeting opportunity. (He added *adequate*.)

There is no limit to what can be accomplished, so long as no one cares who gets the credit for it.

The highest compliment you can pay someone is to listen to them.

NJC surrounded himself with young people and stayed young himself. He married a woman twenty years younger than himself, creating a fabulous marriage and relationship. He surrounded himself with everything that his youthful bride contributed (namely, ideas, friends, energy, even a new son who became his pride and joy).

Each of us will answer for the good we do *not* do.

The whole time I knew him, NJC was always committed to what he referred to as "psychic income" and made daily deposits to his account.

NJC always did what had to be done, before it had to be done and more than what was merely required.

There will always be dirty dishes in the sink.

To *have* a friend you must first *be* a friend.

When my house needs painting and I have plenty of money, I hire someone to get the paint and paint the house for me. When my house needs painting and I don't have extra money to spend, I pick out and buy the paint myself and paint the house myself. Either way, my house gets painted when it needs it.

"If you can, fill the unforgiving minute with sixty seconds worth of distance, and run."[141]

---

[141]"This quote is one of my favorites," he wrote to me. "It's by Kipling, and he is saying that with every minute that you are given, make the absolute most of it that you can. *Unforgiving minute* refers to the fact that every single minute is 60 seconds long—no more, and no less."

When hit with an objection, state, "I can appreciate that. I understand that." Then use the right-angle approach, which is using a new way to restate what you intended. For example, in sales, you're at the end of the sale, and the prospect asks a question, the answer to which is positive. Instead of answering the question, you go right off at a right angle by saying, "If we can [do that], will you [buy] today?"

Do not use the word *but*. It contradicts the other person's statement. Use *sure*, *in addition to*, or *also* instead.

Listen Loudly.

In the land of the blind, the one-eyed man is king.

"An adult is a person of any age who does what rightly must be done, whether they like it or not, without selfish hope of reward." This was told to Neil by his teacher, Dr. Serota, in grade school. He kept it with him his whole life.

"Oh, the gift, the gift they gee us. If only we could see us as others see us." This was one of his favorites.

To change a habit, it cannot be flung out the window. It has to be coaxed down the stairs, one step at a time.

All too often, we make more money on the deals we *don't* do than on the deals we *do* do. When in doubt, pass.

"Remember, Sandy," he said, "revenge is a dish best served cold."

Sandy, you are bigger than anything that can happen to you. Sorrow, misfortune, and suffering are outside your door. You are in the house, and you have the key. Don't let any of them in.

LETTER AND POEM TO RICHARD

Richard and I first met at sleep-away camp when we were 8 years old. We bonded instantly and became lifelong best friends, sharing a lifelong walk together that was legendary by many standards. We shared many things in common, but had others that were different. However, we melded and often acknowledged to each other that we were better together than apart. What follows is a self-explanatory letter that I wrote to him in 2009.

F. SANFORD MAHR
27 August 2009

RHG:

My Brother from another mother, My Fellow Comrade in Arms:

There are times in a man's life when many things come together like a convergence of multiple dots or points, if you will, and he sees things in a way that others may not. However, it doesn't matter, because the fact is, he sees them his way.

Days may have special meanings for some, based on paradigms, customs, or traditions. There are those people, though, who choose to blaze their own trails, creating and leaving their signatures on previously blank pages—or, if you will, their footprints on fresh snow or uninterrupted sands. Oh, the trails we have blazed together, my man! Oh, the footprints left on sand and snow!

Thank you for walking with me through this life and probably others as my "comrade in arms."

Thank you for being my family. However, above being my family, you are *truly* my *friend*.

I had two identical amulets created by a Canadian jewelry artist for the two of us to wear. (One for you and one for me.)

There are no others like them anywhere in the world. They are unique, as is our friendship, brotherhood, and bond. "This, too, shall pass" (Hebrew: גם זה יעבור, *gam zeh yaavor*) is a phrase that occurs in a folktale involving King Solomon. It mostly appears on rings and is signified by the acronym of the three Hebrew letters ג ז י. There are many kabbalistic implications and metaphors surrounding the saying. However, in modern times in this country, perhaps it was made most popular by Abraham Lincoln. "This, too, shall pass" and the associated stories about it were made popular by him in his Address Before the Wisconsin State Agricultural Society, in Milwaukee, on September 30, 1859, where he was quoted as saying:

> It is said an Eastern monarch once charged his wise men to invent him a sentence, to be ever in view, and which should be true and appropriate in all times and situations. They presented him the words: "And this, too, shall pass." How much it expresses. How chastening in the hour of pride. How consoling in the depths of affliction.
>
> —A. Lincoln

Figure 22: This Too Shall Pass

we are...
6.June.2014

we are...
yes, we are
richard gorbaty/sanford mahr
brothers then, brothers now,
brothers still to be....
the walk
the ride
the trails
the journey....
us
in many directions
on many paths
through many times
together then, now, and still to be....
we have laughed
we have cried
we have lived
we have died
oh,
and we live again
don't you know
don't you see
sure, not always in lockstep nor pace,
not always sharing place,
always tho in symbiotic resonance,
backs covered,
vibrating to a harmony few other than we
can nor will,
understand
or for that matter, ever care to....
hah....

were we the same,
there would be no spark,
there would be no flame,
if so,
then the giving we give each,
that which each gains by the presence of each,
would otherwise limit our evolution through
the lives we have lived....
don't you know
don't you see
yes
there is the you
yes
there is the me
yes
there has, nay
there always will be
we
we are....
yes, we are
richard gorbaty/sanford mahr
brothers then, brothers now, brothers still to be....
don't you know
don't you see
sanford mahr/richard gorbaty
brothers for eternity.......

EAGLES AND DUCKS

It is only crowded and competitive at the bottom and middle. The top is wide open.

—Solomon "Sol" Mahr

The top is where Eagles soar.

—F. Sanford Mahr

When you think of eagles, what do you picture?

Are they strong, independent, powerful, proactive beings that soar in the skies?

Don't they live up high, where they are reputed to fly above storms?

And then there are the ducks. When you think of ducks, what do you picture?

Aren't they wedded to the Earth for the most part, waddling around in groups, sometimes off to their little ponds, where they quack, quack, quack most of the time?

Don't quack like a duck; soar like an eagle.

—Ken Blanchard[142]

---

[142]Available from https://en.wikipedia.org/wiki/Ken_Blanchard/.

Figure 23: No Ducks

Metaphorically speaking, eagles and ducks can apply to categories-of people as well. The eagles soar on their own, seizing the possibilities of each moment and making things happen. They find out how to get things done. The ducks, on the other hand, often they stay by their pond. They are unable to soar because they choose to stay grounded. For the most part, they do things the way they have always done them, finding excuses for why they are unable to create more opportunities for themselves. Rather, they find reasons for all the things they *cannot* do.

As a committed eagle, aspire to operate in a Duck Free Zone. You will encounter them, but when you do, recognize them as ducks, and realize that you can never send them to Eagle School.[143]

---

[143]Borrowed from Mac Anderson, *You Can't Send a Duck to Eagle School.* Available at https://www.simpletruths.com/personal-inspiration/you-cant-send-a-duck-to-eagle-school.html/.

THE GOOD MORNING SUN

by F. Sanford Mahr
Written at Chalk Creek, Colorado
a campground at the base of a very large hill
(most assuredly a *Hill Where Excellence Dwells*)

Late last night, the light of day
had finally given way
to black,
white,
luminescent sparkles,
and hues of gray.

Memory served as a mirror,
reflecting moments of connection,
fleeting,
uncertain,
perhaps meant to be dear.

Then there was a thought,
like a crackle of a spark from the fire.
Or was that a moonbeam racing through the air?

What was it about that thought that is true,
This day, this night, no longer blue?

The night sky has become a painting to behold,
But it's the fantasy of what the good morning sun could provide
that beckons like a chest filled with treasure
of diamonds,
of rubies,
and things more precious than gold.

BE | DO | HAVE

Excellence dwells on the hill, where negativity, worry, fear, and doubt are barred from visitation or occupancy.

—F. Sanford Mahr

Ciao | Adios | Lehitraot
2021

BIBLIOGRAPHY

I make no assertion nor assumption of being a master or having created something that is worthwhile and new. I am, however, an acknowledged student of many Masters.

—F. Sanford Mahr

Aczel, Amir D. *Entanglement.* New York: Four Walls Eight Windows, 2001.

Anderson, Mac. *You Can't Send a Duck to Eagle School.* Available at https://www.simpletruths.com/personal-inspiration/you-cant-send-a-duck-to-eagle-school.html/.

Bach, David. *The Automatic Millionaire.* New York: Crown, 2003.

Bach, Richard. *Illusions.* New York: Dell, 1977.

Brande, Dorothea. *Wake Up and Live.* New York: Penguin, 1936.

Campbell, Joseph. *The Inner Reaches of Outer Space.* New York: A. van der Marck, 1986.

Castaneda, Carlos. *The Teachings of Don Juan.* New York: Washington Square Press, 1968.

Chaudhuri, Haridas. *Being, Evolution and Immortality.* Wheaton, IL: Theosophical Publishing House, 1988.

Chilton, David. *The Wealthy Barber.* Roseville, CA: Prima Publishing, 1998.

Chopra, Deepak. *The Deeper Wound.* New York: Harmony Books, 2001.

Covey, Stephen. *The Seven Habits of Highly Effective People and First Things First.* New York: Simon and Schuster, 1989.

Covey, Stephen. *The Seven Habits of Highly Successful People.* New York: Simon and Schuster, 1989.

Csikszentmihalyi, Mihaly. *Flow.* New York: HarperCollins, 1991.

Dobbin, Rabbi Joel C. *The Astrological Secrets of the Hebrew Sages.* New York: Inner Traditions, 1983.

Dyer, Wayne. *Being in Balance.* Available at https://www.hayhouse.com/.

Evans, Nicholas. *The Horse Whisperer.* New York: Delacorte Press, 1995.

Gibran, Kahlil. *The Prophet.* New York: Knopf, 1923.

Goleman, Daniel. *Emotional Intelligence.* New York: Bantam, 1995.

Hill, Napoleon. *Grow Rich with Peace of Mind.* New York: Penguin, 1967.

Hill, Napoleon. *Think and Grow Rich.* Meridian, CT: The Ralston Society, 1937.

Hogan, Bill. *How Do You Eat an Elephant? One Bite at a Time.* Plantation, FL: Llumina Press, 2011.

Hopkins, Tom. *How to Master the Art of Selling.* Issaqua, WA: Made for Success Publishing, 1979.

Jacobson, Simon. *The Wisdom of the Rebbe Menachem Mendel Schneerson.* New York: William Morrow, 1995.

Jordan, David Star. *The Philosophy of Despair.* Cambridge, MA: Harvard University Library, 1902.

Kiyosaki, Robert T. *Rich Dad Poor Dad.* New York: Warner Books, 1997.

Kushner, Harold S. *When Bad Things Happen to Good People.* New York: Schocken Books, 1981.

Lombardo, Elizabeth. *A Happy You: Your Ultimate Prescription for Happiness.* Garden City, NY: Morgan James, 2010.

Maller, Rabbi Allen S. *God, Sex and Kabbalah.* Los Angeles: Ridgefield Publishing Company, 1983.

Maltz, Maxwell. *Psycho-Cybernetics.* New York: Penguin Random House, 2015.

Maxwell, John C. *The Success Journey: The Process of Living Your Dreams.* Nashville, TN: Thomas Nelson, 1997.

Millman, Dan. *Way of the Peaceful Warrior.* Novato, CA: New World Library, 2000.

Nietzsche, Friedrich. *Twilight of the Idols.* Trans. Duncan Large. Oxford: Oxford University Press, 2003. (Originally published in 1888.)

Nin, Anaïs. *The Diary of Anaïs Nin*, vol. 3: 1939–1944. New York: Harcourt Brace Jovanovich, 1996.

Roosevelt, Eleanor. *This Is My Story.* New York: Simon & Schuster, 1937.

Schlatter, John Wayne. *Gifts by the Side of the Road.* Salem, OR: Heart Productions and Publishing, 2012.

Silverstein, Shel. *The Giving Tree.* New York: Harper & Row, 1964.

Sinek, Simon. *Find Your Why: A Practical Guide for Finding Purpose for You and Your Team.* New York: Penguin, 2017.

Stanley, Thomas J., and Danko, William D. *The Millionaire Next Door*. Lanham, MD: Taylor Trade Publishing, 1996.

Toffler, Alvin. *Future Shock*. New York: Random House, 1970.

Walsch, Neale Donald. *Conversations with God*. New York: Penguin Putnam, 1996.

Made in the USA
Columbia, SC
15 May 2021

38005928R00119